PRAISE FOR

Love Unbroken

A harrowingly honest narrative of trauma, suffering and addiction, *Love Unbroken* is also a triumphant story of soul redemption— redemption not as a final event but as an ongoing process aided by surrender, love, grace, spiritual humility and also by Amazonian plant medicine. This courageous tale helps us question our unexamined assumptions about drugs, drug addicts, addiction, and treatment.
—GABOR MATÉ M.D., author of *In The Realm of Hungry Ghosts: Close Encounters With Addiction*

I could not stop reading Susan Thesenga's *Love Unbroken*. It is stirring, riveting, humbling, and heart opening. The details may be specific to her own life, but the revelations are for us all. May it benefit many!
—GANGAJI, contemporary American spiritual teacher, author of *Hidden Treasure: Finding the Truth in Your Life Story*

Love Unbroken is, on one level, a harrowing account, written with great sensitivity and honesty, of addiction, loss and despair. On another level, it both points to and expresses the unconditional and indestructible love that shines at the heart of all experience when everything else has been broken or lost. On every page one feels that Susan Thesenga is being stripped bare but, at the same time, being taken more and more deeply into this love. The reader cannot help but feel both the heartbreak and the love that shines underneath it.
—RUPERT SPIRA, non-dual teacher, and author of *The Transparency of Things*

Love Unbroken not only tells it like it is—giving us a very real picture of addiction—it also offers help and hope to those caught in the disease and to their family members who suffer along with the addict. The story is compelling, and the spiritual message is uplifting. The unusual story of Pamela's recovery should interest all those who are open-minded about how addicts can recover.

> —JOHN GIORDANO, C.C.J.S., MAC, CAP, founder
> of G&G Holistic Addictions Treatment Program in
> N. Miami Beach, Florida

Beautifully written! *Love Unbroken* is the riveting story of one family's journey through the torments of addiction. It gives us a window into the life of a young woman who spent years on the streets and struggled with relentless mental illness. It also gives us a window into her spiritual awakening, and the bonds of loving that grow ever more deep and clear within her family. Filled with wisdom and hope, this book will touch all who seek true freedom.

> —TARA BRACH, PH.D., Teacher of Buddhist
> Mindfulness and author of *Radical Acceptance*

Love Unbroken speaks to humankind's opportunity to discover its true expression as love in action. It will serve to foster the medicines of non-judgment and compassion that all facets of society crave.

> —MUKTI GRAY, Spiritual Teacher, Open Gate Sangha

When do we give up on our children? When have we reached the end of our rope? In *Love Unbroken* Thesenga answers these questions with "Never." This is a true story of how love can survive in the midst of betrayal, disappointment, and addiction. The book is written from the heart and poignantly touches on the many perils along the path to recovery.

> —MATT FLICKSTEIN, Director of Forestway, author of
> *Journey to the Center* and *Meditator's Atlas: A Roadmap
> to the Inner World*

A compelling story about a young woman's struggle with addiction and the healing she received working with *ayahuasca*, described by the author as "the only medicine strong enough to break through Pamela's deep despair and self-loathing." *Love Unbroken* needs to be widely read.

—RICK DOBLIN, PH.D, Founder and Executive Directive of MAPS (Multidisciplinary Association for Psychedelic Studies, a non-profit research and education organization)

The longer I study addiction, the more I realize that I'm really studying trauma; sometimes psychological, physical, or sexual, and too often all three. Research suggests that ayahuasca can allow individuals to address unresolved trauma from their past, providing a renewed sense of hope, self-worth, and understanding. *Love Unbroken* is a story of pain and loss eventually overcome by self-discovery, love and compassion with the help of one of mankind's most fascinating plant medicines: *ayahuasca*.

—PHILIPPE LUCAS M.A., Research Affiliate, Center for Addictions Research of BC; Coordinator, Observational Study of Ayahuasca-Assisted Addictions Therapy

Breaking the cycle of addiction is not always about choice. The rainforest alkaloid *ibogaine* gives those who want to choose an opportunity to make that break. Pam Thesenga gives the reader an insiders first hand account of this journey home.

— DEBORAH C. MASH, PH.D., Professor of Neurology, Miller School of Medicine, Miami, FL

LOVE

UNBROKEN

ALSO BY SUSAN THESENGA:

The Undefended Self

love
unbroken

from addiction to redemption

by

SUSAN THESENGA

and

Pamela Thesenga

BEING &
AWAKENING

CHARLOTTESVILLE

FIRST EDITION • APRIL 2012
BEING AND AWAKENING, LLC
www.loveunbroken.org

© Copyright 2012 Susan Thesenga

Love Unbroken is a work of nonfiction.
Some names and identifying details have been changed.

ISBN: 9780615559803
Library of Congress Control Number:
2011942499

DESIGN & TYPOGRAPHY:
D. Patrick Miller • Fearless Literary Services
www.fearlessbooks.com

Table of Contents

Dedication

*For all the suffering addicts
and the suffering parents of addicts*

Prologue

Heartbreak

Opening to whatever is present can be a heartbreaking business. But let the heart break, for your breaking heart only reveals a core of love unbroken.

—Gangaji, contemporary spiritual teacher,
from *A Diamond in your Pocket*

This is a true story of the greatest heartbreak of my life. My heart was broken open by witnessing my adopted daughter Pamela's ten-year descent into the depths of the disease of drug addiction. For three of those years she fell to the very bottom of the bottom—living on the streets, sleeping under bridges and eating out of dumpsters.

Pamela had been a disturbed child, but addiction further shattered her dignity and destroyed her fragile self-worth. I had been a loving mother and a competent professional, but the devastation of my daughter shredded my self-confidence and made me question every-thing I knew. As our inner certainties crumbled and our hearts were broken, our outer lives lurched from crisis to crisis.

And yet… passing through the destruction of who we thought we were brought surprising healing, as we humbly opened to the redemp-tive presence of unconditional love.

Welcome to our unusual love story.

Susan Thesenga
March 2012

CHAPTER 1

This Should Never Have Happened!

Virginia, December 1994

I AM awakened at 3:00 a.m. on a cold mid-December morning by my thirteen-year-old daughter Pamela. She thrusts a phone receiver into my hand. I sputter in protest, but she insists I take it. She retreats to the door of my bedroom, giving me a backward glance. She looks scared.

It's my friend Kate, whose first words are: "Pamela has been raped." The words make no sense.

"But she's right here with me. What are you talking about?"

As Kate provides more details, her words slowly penetrate the fog of my sleepiness and the shock that is spreading through my body. I repeat her words to make sure I'm hearing correctly: "You're telling me that tonight, while I was asleep, Pam left our house, got in a car with three boys, and was raped by all three of them, and then they brought her back home?"

"Yes," Kate confirms, "that's what she told me. I'm so sorry... so sorry. Go, be with Pam now, and I'll talk to you later."

I hang up, shaking, disoriented. I look around, distressed. Where is my husband? Where is *Donovan*? Slowly it dawns on me that Donovan is in Brazil, teaching, and isn't due back for another week. I feel heartsick, bereft.

Pam is still hovering in the doorway. I ask her to sit on the bed. I notice her hair has been cut, bizarrely. In fact, it has been almost chopped off completely.

"What did you do to your hair?"

"I cut it," she says, hanging her head and looking embarrassed.

Awkward silence. Then I ask, "How did Kate find out about this?"

"I called her."

"Why?"

Her words tumble out, and I'm relieved that she's talking. "I was so scared and upset when I got back. I changed my clothes. I felt so dirty. I didn't know what to do next. Then I remembered that book you gave me, *Our Bodies, Ourselves,* that book about everything for women. It had a chapter on ..." she falters "... on what happened tonight. It said it wasn't my fault and that I should call a friend. So I called Kate. She told me to wake you up, but I felt too scared to do that, so she said she would talk to you for me if I gave you the phone."

"Okay, Pam, I'm glad you called her." I'm doing everything I can to focus my mind on what she's saying, but inside my head all I can hear are the high-pitched screams of my own denial: *No, no, no, this can't have happened. No, no, no, I don't want to hear it.*

I attempt a deep breath and find it catches in my chest. I force out the words: "Now, please, tell me in your words what happened to you tonight."

"James was scratching at my window and insisting I come out." She stops, regarding me warily.

"Who is James?" I ask, confused. "Why was he scratching at your window?"

"He's a boy from school."

"How old is he?"

"I don't know, maybe sixteen or seventeen."

My mind is racing. I remember that her homeroom teacher, a friend of ours, has recently told us that Pam has been flirting with a lot of boys, including older high school kids, and getting a bad reputation. My body shudders at the recollection. The shrill voice of my inner critic shouts: *How could you have let this happen? Why didn't you take stronger measures to control her? How could you have failed to educate her about the dangers of going out with boys she doesn't know?*

Struggling to keep my balance despite the harsh voice in my head, I do everything I can to appear calm. I know from experience that she'll clam up otherwise.

"He knows where you live?"

"Yes."

"Because you told him where you live?"

"Yes."

I sigh, unable to stop myself. "Why did you go out with him?"

"He was scratching with his fingernails. I thought it was a knife. I thought he would hurt me if I didn't go."

That's it. I can't contain my response. "Pam, that doesn't make any sense! If you thought a boy outside your window was going to hurt you, why wouldn't you come to get me?"

"I was scared to tell you. Then you wouldn't let me go."

"Okay, that sounds more true. Where did you think you were going?"

"He said he was going to take me to a party in Charlottesville." Pam is getting more and more agitated.

I try to soothe her. "Pam, you don't need to say any more now, not until you're ready. I'm so sorry this happened, so sorry." I'm trying to be the adult here, but once again my shock is too near the surface; I can't contain it. "Oh, my God," I breathe, my head in my hands. "I can't believe you got in the car with them."

"See, you're going to blame me. I knew it! You think I'm really bad." She runs to the door of the room, pauses, and glances back furtively. Then, quietly, almost as an afterthought, she looks right at me and says, "You're just too old. You'll never understand." She pauses, then adds in a challenging tone, "And, anyway, you're not my real mother!"

I stand up and move slowly toward her, speaking softly, attempting reassurance.

"I'm sorry, Pam. I know you're upset. So am I. Of course it wasn't your fault, just like the book says. You were raped. What these boys did was very wrong. And I know you have trouble accepting me as your mother, but I am your mother, and I am so sorry this happened."

I'm about three feet from her now, and she's softened a little. But now my own composure is cracking and I sputter, "It's just hard for me to believe. Didn't you know it was a very risky thing to get into a car with three boys in the middle of the night?"

As soon as the question is out of my mouth, I regret it. I know she already feels awful—how can I keep pushing her? But really, how could she be so horribly, dangerously naive? I know my daughter has been acting strange these last few months; her secretive behavior started escalating when she entered seventh grade at the local public school, after spending three years at a small private school. But I had no earthly idea she could be so reckless.

☙

Always hanging like a grey smog in the back of my mind, clouding my vision of her, is the sad story of Pam's early trauma. My daughter had a soul-shattering infancy. She was abandoned by her alcoholic, schizophrenic mother at eight months and lived in an orphanage, then in foster care, until we were able to adopt her at eleven months.

We knew she had serious psychological problems when we first met her in the visiting room of the social services department. She could not make eye contact and avoided being held. She was terrified of loud noises and of men. She moved slowly, and we thought for a while she might even be retarded. Later we had her tested and found she had an average IQ, but probably suffered from Fetal Alcohol Effects because of her mother's use of drugs and alcohol during pregnancy. This was confirmed when she was in third grade and was absolutely unable to learn multiplication tables; certain logical parts of her brain simply didn't function.

Puberty and other challenges of adolescence began for Pam long before she was even officially a teenager. By ten she was distrustful and defiant, by eleven she was lying and hiding, and by twelve she was obsessed with boys and sex. At age twelve she'd had a sexual encounter in Brazil with a boy who teased and egged her on. We had hoped it was an isolated incident, but now it seemed she was wildly flirtatious with older boys at her school. At a school social event Donovan and I attended, a boy came up to us and sneered, "Do you know that your daughter has kissed just about every boy in this school?"

She seemed to be gravitating to the most morally debased and disturbed kids in her class. Recently, when we'd picked her up from the roller skating rink, she had proudly informed us that some of the girls were teaching her how to spit and fight. After that, we'd decided there would be no more roller skating.

❧

Now, in the aftermath of what I've just learned, I'm overcome with anger that those boys were so cruel and that she acted so stupidly. I feel guilt for having failed to get through to my daughter, and I'm dumbfounded that we didn't see what was coming. As these feelings swirl inside, it's hard for me to hear Pam's response, much less imagine the state of mind in which she could blithely say:

"I don't know, Mom, I just wanted to have fun. They said we were going to a party."

My mind freezes. "*You just wanted to have fun,*" I mumble. How can this be? Who is this girl who can't see he difference between fun and danger? I have no idea what goes on in her head. I'm drowning.

I struggle back to the surface, paddling madly to come to grips with what is happening, to move toward action. "Okay, okay. Oh, my God. We have to call the police and report this. Rape is a crime. These boys will probably be arrested."

I call the police. Pam doesn't want to talk anymore, so we go to the living room and wait for them to show up. When they arrive—two middle-aged white men with bellies bulging over the belts of their police suits—Pam describes the three boys. All are African-American, one slightly older than the other two. James, the boy at the window, was the one with whom she had flirted most heavily; and he was the cruelest to her. She describes the oldest one as almost nice. He seemed to be the only one who was aware that what they were doing was wrong and was concerned about how she was doing—even as he joined the others in forcing himself on her.

The police ask what she was wearing at the time, and she produces some skimpy underwear and a mini-mini-skirt that she confesses she'd cut down. It would barely cover her butt, and it's freezing outside. I'm embarrassed when she shows it to the cop. With a careful lack of expression, they take it for evidence.

At their suggestion, we drive to the hospital emergency room so that evidence can be gathered. Hot waves of shame surge through me. I'm almost gasping for breath, unable to slow or deepen my breathing. In an effort to regain some semblance of calm, I sing to myself—again and again—these lines from a Brazilian hymn:

Firmeza, firmeza no amor	Firmness, firmness in love
Firmeza, firmeza aonde estou	Firmness, firmness where I am

As I pray for inner firmness, a small measure of calm trickles into my body by the time we arrive at the hospital.

✤

Pam writes:

The night of the rape is a night I remember very well.

I talk to James, and he says that he and some of his friends are going to pick me up so we can go into Charlottesville to hang out. I have to sneak out because my mom would never let me go. I get all ready, wearing a little skirt that I had cut to make shorter. I have some kind of obsession with cutting, which would become extreme later, in my meth addiction. I still don't fully understand it. I have also cut my hair by myself, really butchering it. They arrive and park a ways down the road, so I sneak out to meet them. I get in the car. There are three of them.

They're drinking and smoking pot, which they offer to me. They say we're going into town by a back way, but I know it isn't the way to get there. When we stop on a dark road in the middle of nowhere, I begin to get a little worried. They say they want to have sex with me. All of them. I say no, and they keep pulling at my skirt and poking me with their long nails. James takes me out of the car and tells me just to have sex with them. I again say I don't want to. He tells me if I don't, they will leave me out in the cold where we are and take my clothes. He shows me a bullet to a gun he says is in the trunk. I'm scared and confused and feel like I should have to do it because I went with them. I just didn't know what I was getting into.

But I still say no. They eventually push themselves on me, one at a time, in the car. The older one seems more aware of what he's doing than the others, and is as nice as someone forcing someone to have sex with them can be, I guess. Finally they finish and drive me home.

As I get out of the car, they ask if my mom has money in the house. I say I don't know, but I will go look. They tell me to do that and come back out and give them money, or they'll come in and shoot me and my mom. I go into my mom's office and get all the money I can find out of her purse; then I go back out. But they have driven off.

I go inside and I am so scared, so upset. I change my clothes and wonder what to do next. Then I remember this book my mom gave me about women and their bodies. After reading it, I call Kate. Then I give the phone to my mom so Kate can tell her what happened, not me.

The next thing I remember is the hospital. It's awful. They have this kit they have to do. All kinds of tests and stuff. They pull out pubic hair and hair from my head. They swab me and give me pills. They give me an injection in my leg that makes my whole leg hurt so bad I can hardly walk. A counselor comes to talk to me. I don't remember anything she said.

❧

Driving away from the hospital, I keep saying aloud, "This is so awful... I can't believe it." My head feels wrapped in electrified barbed wire, every thought delivering a new shock to my brain. My mind is screaming, "THIS SHOULDN'T HAVE HAPPENED."

Pam, on the other hand, is preternaturally calm. Dissociated, I am sure, but calm nonetheless. She repeats several times: "It happened, Mom, it just happened."

CHAPTER 2

What On Earth Can We Do Now?

Virginia, December 1994

THE police find the boys, and by mid-January all three are charged with rape and the one over eighteen is taken into custody.

In early March we go to trial. Sitting in the courtroom, I feel embarrassed as my rural, conservative neighbors—the judge, the prosecuting attorney, the public defenders, the boys' families—hear the details of what happened that night. I believe my mothering of this girl has been woefully inadequate. Do my neighbors judge me as much as I judge myself?

I clutch in my hands a small holy card—a picture of Jesus with red and blue rays coming out of his heart—and I pray for some quality of mercy to be brought to these proceedings.

Although I do not consider myself Christian, I see Jesus as an embodiment of unconditional divine love and a teacher on the path of total acceptance and forgiveness. For me Jesus is a spiritual master, directing our attention to realizing the kingdom of heaven within ourselves as he had done. While I now turn to other teachers as well, including Indian sages and Buddhist masters, I could hardly bring a representation of any other archetype of divine love into that rural Virginia county courtroom.

When Donovan and I went before the county planning commission nearly twenty years earlier to get a special use permit to start a center for personal growth on our land, we tried to impress the locals that we were God-fearing people by explaining that the weekend be-fore our appearance at that hearing we'd held both a Passover Seder and an Easter service on our property.

We described our approach to spirituality as non-denomina-tional. To which we were met with the firm, even slightly threatening reminder by a local minister speaking in his slow Southern drawl, "We're denominational around here."

So it is clear that I'd better at least stick to a recognizable Christian image if I am going to bring into that grim setting—where crimes are judged and punishment meted—some reminder of divine forgiveness and mercy.

I listen with a heavy heart to the boys' recitations about my daugh-ter. The two younger ones, whom Pam has described as being espe-cially cruel, repeat that she was known as a "freak," their word for a promiscuous girl. They didn't believe she would object. The older one, who has been in jail since his arrest in January, says he knows what they did was wrong, just not *this* wrong.

Dimly, I'm wondering: *What are these boys really feeling? Do they have any remorse, or do they feel set up by this crazy white girl? Have they internalized the verdict of themselves as 'bad boys'? Will they be able to turn their behavior around, or are they already set on a lifelong path of liv-ing out negative expectations—theirs and others'—about their badness?*

I notice that when I think they blame Pam, I feel angry. On the other hand, when I think they condemn themselves for life, I feel sad. But I have no idea what is really going on in their minds.

Still, I struggle to understand: How did we all end up in this tense, unhappy courtroom and what are we going to take away from it? I know Pam has lived inside a dark hole of self-hatred for years and I fear the rape will push her further into that darkness.

The boys are convicted of the rape. The two underage boys are sent to a juvenile facility, and the one over eighteen is sentenced to prison for a year. The judge has been fair and considerate; the Commonwealth's attorney was kind and solicitous of Pam, gently encouraging her to tell the truth. I am now grateful to my neighbors who have helped assure a just outcome to this ordeal.

At the end of the trial, as the older boy is being led away in his orange jumpsuit, he passes close to me. We lock eyes for a moment, and I spontaneously reach out and offer him the holy card, the image of Jesus. The guard nods assent, and the boy takes the card. I mumble, "God bless you."

Pam leans over to me and whispers, "Oh God, Mom, you are so weird." She's probably right. My passion to see the good in everyone can verge on insipid Pollyanna optimism. My attachment to believing there's a potential happy ending for every story can lead me to be unwilling to see what's in front of me. Nowhere would my determination to see goodness and my desire for happy endings become more evident than in my journey with Pamela.

🦚

Shortly after the rape, we enter family therapy with Dr. Curry, a highly trained and recommended psychologist who also sees Pam individually. This is familiar territory for Pam; she has been in therapy several times before in her life.

When she was four years old, she had a brief but devastating incident of sexual abuse with a stranger. Pam was shocked. Donovan was furious. I was horrified. We immediately got her into play therapy, which lasted a year. She calmed down some, but the therapist warned us that the effects of this abuse would resurface in adolescence.

When she was ten years old, Pam received an unexpected phone call from her biological mother who had found our number and called repeatedly—hanging up whenever Donovan or I picked up the phone—until Pam answered. Her mother announced, "Do you know who this is? I am your real mother, and I love you. Those people you live with aren't your real parents." I was in the room, and I saw the distress on Pam's face—she looked stricken. I insisted on taking the phone out of her hand. The line went dead, but the damage had been done. So once again, at our insistence, Pam reluctantly went into therapy for a year with a woman who told me that she really liked Pam and she found our daughter unusually self-aware for someone so young. The therapist added, "Pam will grow into a really interesting adult… that is, if she survives adolescence."

A year later, our babysitter found a suicide note Pam had crumpled up and left in the wastebasket. We took it seriously, immediately picked her up from school, and went to see a psychiatrist. She went through several months of talk therapy, which ended after the doctor convinced us that Pam had never been serious about suicide.

Now, our family therapist assures us that Pam is handling her feelings about the rape well. We begin to suspect that Dr. Curry may not be getting the real story when she tells us Pam has good friends who understand her. We know this isn't true. In fact, after the rape, Pam's only real friend at school tells Pam that her mother has forbidden her to associate with our daughter anymore because of Pam's bad reputation.

We know all too well how easy it is for Pam to lie convincingly; she has even told us that it's easier for her to lie than to tell the truth. It appears to me that Pam is successfully conning Dr. Curry. Pam's prior exposure to therapy has given her just the right words to say to fool any therapist into thinking she's coping well. I expect Pam sees this as the shortest route to getting Dr. Curry off her back.

At home Pam seems numb, even somewhat robotic. I try to reach over the terrible wall of her isolation with assurances of my love and acceptance. But my words are like thin twine thrown over a fortified barricade, not nearly substantial enough for her to scale the walls of her inner prison.

I try to tell Dr. Curry that Pam is much more disturbed than she realizes, that she's probably making up stories any therapist would want to hear. But Dr. Curry tells me—in effect—to back off, reminding me that my anxiety is my own issue. Pam keeps saying that she wants to put the rape behind her. The therapist is convinced; I'm not.

Looking back over all the therapy we've arranged for Pam and how she has responded to it, Donovan and I realize that she's never gotten much out of any of it. We have also tried to introduce Pam to the spiritual work we've taught for the last twenty years—the Pathwork.[1] But the concepts were way beyond her comprehension and her capacity for self-reflection was not well enough developed to undertake the rigors of examining her thoughts and feelings. Nor did she have the self-discipline to sit in quiet meditation. We are at a loss. Our daughter remains in turmoil, and she clearly needs more help than she's getting.

What on earth can we do for her now?

---

[1] The Pathwork is a psychological-spiritual discipline for personal transformation that we've taught for over twenty years, which is summarized in my book *The Undefended Self.* For more information, see *www.pathwork.org.* We have taught this work primarily at the spiritual center we founded in 1972—Sevenoaks Retreat Center—which is located on 130 acres in the foothills of the Blue Ridge mountains, where we still live and work. See *www.sevenoaksretreat.org* or *www.sevenoakspathwork.org.*

CHAPTER 3

Rainforest Sacrament

Traveling to Brazil, April 1995

SHATTERED by the rape, drained by the trial and disappointed with our family therapy, all we want to do is get far, far away. We decide to take a family vacation to Brazil during Pam's spring break. We have visited Brazil often and have come to love this warm and welcoming country where doors have opened wide for us.

Like children with skinned knees, we are fleeing into the arms of Mother Brazil, a country whose heart-centered culture feels like a soothing balm to our wounded North American psyches. We are eager to dig more deeply into Brazilian culture—a rich mix of African, Amazonian, and European traditions—from which have emerged many uniquely Brazilian spiritual flowers.

Donovan and I have been working as therapists and teachers in Brazil, traveling there three times a year for each of the last two years. We are working at the invitation of a Brazilian psychologist, training therapists in the Pathwork, the psychological-spiritual work we've been teaching in the U.S. for many years. Our work is being very well received in Brazil and our three books about the Pathwork are about to be published in Portuguese.

Every time we come to Brazil to teach, we also visit a spiritual community located in Visconde de Mauá, a mountain valley outside Rio de Janeiro. We have come to know this particular community well and have become friends with its leader, Dr. José Rosa, a Brazilian psychiatrist.

Pamela has accompanied us during several visits, beginning when she was eleven years old. At the end of her first visit, on the bus ride to the airport, she started sobbing: "I love Brazil. I don't want to leave. I want to live here." She's eager to join us again.

The community is part of a Brazilian church called the *Santo Daime* (loosely translated as "holy gift"), which began in the Amazon rain forest but has spread throughout Brazil. During our visits to the community, Donovan and I have participated in many powerful spiritual ceremonies. José is teaching us the ways of this unusual church, which reflect the Brazilian multicultural approach to spirituality. The church has its roots in native Amazonian shamanism, but also incorporates Christian, African, and Spiritist elements. We are returning now in real need of our own healing from the traumas of the last few months, and also hoping for more clarity about how to help Pam.

🙈

In the airport waiting for our flight to Rio de Janeiro, Pam announces, "I want to drink *Daime*." Donovan and I look hard at each other instead of answering her. We are both thinking: *Could we, dare we, risk having Pam drink the sacrament that is central to the spiritual ceremonies that have meant so much to us?*

After Pam and I are settled in our seats in the airplane, I lean over to her and say, "We'll have to talk to José about whether or not it's right for you to drink the *Daime*."[1]

---

[1] "*Dai-me*" is a Portuguese word pronounced "Die-may." The word literally means "Give me," which is a shorthand for the plea, "Give me love, give me strength, give me light," often repeated in the prayers and hymns of the church. In English "*Daime*" is usually (mis)pronounced as either "Dime" or "Die-me."

The *Daime* is the name given to *ayahuasca* when it is taken as a sacrament within the church ceremonies. *Ayahuasca* is a psychoactive tea made from brewing together two jungle plants. It has been used for millennia by the shamans of indigenous cultures throughout the Amazon basin, which consider this tea a healing gift from the gods.

The *Santo Daime* church, which began in the Amazon region of Brazil in the 1930s, regards the ceremonial use of *ayahuasca* in the same way wine is viewed by Christian churches in the ritual of communion. During communion, wine is believed to transform into the blood of Christ. In a similar way, the *Santo Daime* church—fully legal in Brazil—believes its sacrament to be a living spiritual teacher.

While it may be difficult for most civilized North Americans to embrace the idea that a plant could be a teacher for humans, it is very common for native peoples throughout the world to regard certain plants with psychedelic properties as gifts from spirit for healing the soul and teaching humans a better way of life. Such plants and plant mixtures have been called *entheogens*, a word indicating that these plants have a capacity to induce a felt connection to the divine mystery.[2]

It is common in some indigenous *ayahuasca* ceremonies, as well as in services in the Brazilian *Daime* church, for children to participate (at their own level) along with adults. Adolescents are often given

---

[2]Dr. Andrew Weil—noted authority on wellness and natural medicines—writes in 1972, "Every human being is born with an innate drive to experience altered states of consciousness." He affirms that certain mind-altering drugs which help humans achieve nonordinary awareness (the same substances which were later called *entheogens*) can be used in positive ways. He uses as an example: "Amazonian Indians use natural drugs in natural ways, surrounding their use with ritual, relying on the supervision of experts qualified by their own experience, and applying the states of consciousness to positive ends." (page 195 of *The Natural Mind.*) The *Santo Daime* evolved from the traditions of these Amazonian Indians. See also the research of Harvard botanist Richard Schultes in *Plants of the Gods.*

this drink as part of their initiation ceremony. So it is not out of the question that Pam could drink the sacrament.

❧

Secretly, I am thrilled that Pam wants to join us in a *Daime* ceremony. Donovan and I know that drinking this sacrament in the context of sacred ceremony has changed our own lives for the better. We have had our minds expanded, our bodies purged, our spirits ignited. We have both been on a spiritual path for thirty years, but nothing else has taken us to such deep levels of consciousness as participating in these ceremonies. We have explored everything from Zen Buddhist meditation retreats to psychotherapy to bio-energetic bodywork to the Pathwork, the discipline in which we have immersed ourselves for the last two decades. All our prior inner work prepared a solid and resilient platform from which we dived deep into this unusual path. We know the *Daime* has been good for us.

But we have our doubts about giving it to Pam. Here we are—the parents of a deeply disturbed thirteen-year-old American girl, whose biological mother was addicted to drugs and alcohol—seriously contemplating giving our daughter a powerful psychoactive Amazonian jungle brew. **For her healing!** We're well aware that most Americans would consider us irresponsible, if not insane.

I am driven by a strong desire to help Pam with the traumas of the rape and her early abuse. I know that nothing we have offered her in the States—neither personal nor family therapy, nor the rape crisis counseling she briefly attended—has begun to touch the depth of her issues. At the same time, I am apprehensive that the intensity of drinking *Daime* could fragment her already very fragile personality. I have no idea what impact it might have on her propensity toward addiction. She is only a child, whereas Donovan and I have fully formed adult egos. We have worked on ourselves for years. Pam has only the beginning of an idea about what it means to look at herself and probe inside for what is motivating her behavior.

Though Donovan and I whisper with each other during our all-night flight to Rio—sharing our hopes as well as our misgivings about giving *Daime* to Pam—we are unable to conclude what would be best for our daughter.

CHAPTER 4

Diving Deep

Flashback to Mauá, Brazil,
January 1993 – December 1993

T HE long flight to Brazil gives me time to reflect back on our first
year of drinking *Daime*, two years earlier.

Donovan first experienced the *Daime* in January 1993 when he
came to the community in Mauá for a month-long workshop led by
Dr. Rosa and Alex Polari, founder of this community and author of
several books about this Brazilian religion.

As workshop leaders ourselves, we often attended those led by
others in our field. But this time was different. Before that workshop,
Donovan was feeling flat, stuck and unhappy. Running Sevenoaks
had ceased being a pleasure, and he felt utterly defeated by his many
failed attempts to stop smoking cigarettes.

Donovan knew he needed something big to release the paralysis in
his life, so he started asking friends for recommendations. One mentioned José Rosa, whom we had met years earlier when he was studying in the United States. "I hear that José is now doing programs in the
Brazilian jungle using shamanic rituals and a strong native psychedelic
drink." This surely sounded exotic enough to Donovan, and he was interested but skeptical. In a phone conversation José told him that the
Daime is not a psychedelic, and is in fact quite different from anything
he might have experienced before. The workshop required a month's
commitment of time, and traveling all the way to Brazil. Donovan's

primary concern was that he might travel all that way and spend all that time and money, only to find that the experience was not strong enough to uncover the roots of his depression or help him with his nicotine addiction.

José suggested that Donovan contact Dr. James Bates, another psychiatrist and an acquaintance of Donovan's, who had experienced the *Daime* a year earlier. Dr. Bates told Donovan that he felt so good about the experience that he was planning to do it again, but also that, "I've never been so terrified in my life as I was in the *Daime* in Brazil." This convinced Donovan to go: if it was terrifying, it could hardly be bland or shallow!

❧

During Donovan's month in Brazil I get several letters from him:

> I've been through three ceremonies now and one thing is clear: The *Daime* is a fierce teacher. The energy that gets generated can be so intense that the temptation to run away is nearly overwhelming. I've experienced some of the terror I was warned about, but the joy and awakening are equally strong. Let me tell you about what happened in my very first work.[1] The center pole that supports the roof of the church was emanating a strong light, so I approached it. The light

---

[1]Each *Daime* ceremony is called a "work," suggesting that they are, indeed, hard work. There are different kinds of works, including 1) *Hinarios*, which are all night dancing works, in which participants dance prescribed steps while singing hymns that have been channeled by the founders and elders of the religion, and 2) Healing Works which involve singing particular hymns aimed at healing the participants, who may lie down to receive their healing, and 3) Concentration works which involve an hour or more of seated quiet contemplation, along with singing certain hymns.

grew stronger and stronger and I could feel waves of love coming from this center pole and into me. The message I heard was: "How wonderful that you heard the call and you came. You are meant to be here." This has sustained me through some difficult times since then....

Last night was work number six. I came to it deeply unhappy about the fact that I'm still smoking. I've been tied to this ball and chain for forty-two years now. The work yesterday was called a Concentration. We drank a large glass of sacrament and then sat in silence for a long time with eyes closed. I fell into a super-deep meditation in which I was shown the clearest view I've had yet of my real self, my true and essential spiritual nature. I could plainly see that my true self does not smoke. More than that, I was shown that smoking pulls me in a direction exactly away from my real self.

As soon as the work ended I threw away my remaining cigarettes. We'll see....

It has been one week since I threw away my nicotine fix, and I have had not the slightest desire to smoke. Please allow me to emphasize that. I have NO DESIRE to smoke. This has never happened before. Some might call this only a minor miracle, but for me it is truly a miracle. My intense nicotine addiction has been utterly removed, like magic, in an instant.

🖋

Several of us meet Donovan at the airport on his return. The glow about him is palpable. He embraces us all and weeps. After twenty-three years of marriage, I feel like I am meeting a new man. I say aloud, "Whatever you got there, I want it too!"

In April 1993, Donovan and I, Pamela's godparents—John and Anne Peterson—eleven-year-old Pamela, the Petersons' four-year-old son Luke, and several other friends go back for a two-week visit. We stay in a comfortable *pousada* (inn) nearby. An American woman in the community takes care of the children so we can experience the *Daime* ceremonies.

During my first work, I am surprised that the drink tastes almost pleasant to me—like peach brandy. I'd heard that it was famous for its foul taste. As I feel the force of the drink arriving, the area around my heart becomes warm, expanded, and relaxed. Through many years of training in the Pathwork and elsewhere, I have learned to hear the still, small voice of spirit within me. And now I "hear" the voice of the *Daime* reassuring me that its intent is only to amplify this inner voice, the universal spiritual teacher within every human being which leads us toward healing and awakening.

Midway through the work, during an extended period of quiet meditation, I hear that inner voice again, only this time it's indeed amplified. It feels like someone is shouting at me through a megaphone! It is clearly speaking to my outer self, saying unequivocally, "Rise and follow me."

But then I question, "Is this a true voice of spirit… or am I making this up?" Then the voice comes again: "Rise and follow me." I hesitate: this is a work in which everyone sits firmly and quietly in their chairs in a circle around the central altar. I don't want to embarrass myself by getting up and leaving my place, following some crazy voice in my head. I go back to meditating by following my breath, hoping the voice will shut up.

It doesn't. I hear again, "Rise and follow me." My resistance collapses.

I feel akin to the fishermen whom Jesus called from their worldly tasks when he invited them to follow Him. My entire adult life has been devoted to the spiritual path. If this is what it has all come to—this moment of being called to leave my chair, to step outside the norms and rules of this particular ceremony, to stand up in an unfamiliar church in a rural community in Brazil where I know almost no one, and to walk out into the night in a foreign terrain where I do not speak the local language—I will do it.

I stand up. I can tell that José Rosa is looking at me with disapproval, but the need to obey the deepest voice I have ever heard is decisive. I know that following this voice is all I can do. So I remain standing. Then the voice speaks again: "Now you may sit down." I do so with relief, feeling that I have somehow passed a test—as it turns out, the first of many tests in the *Daime*—of trusting and surrendering to the inner voice.

In my second work, I feel a sudden breeze, and inwardly I see a picture of the rainforest with a beautiful woman superimposed on it. She announces herself as the Queen of the Forest. She has come from the jungle through the medium of the tea. She makes it clear that she is to be my teacher and my mother. I feel deeply happy that the archetype of the Divine Mother is appearing to me as the Queen of the Forest, and I know that I don't need to do anything at all to receive Her unconditional love. There is nothing I want to do except sit in my place in the church singing songs of praise to the Mother and Her creation.

In my third work, I encounter sheer and prolonged terror, during a twelve-hour session that feels like an eternity. This is an all-night work of singing and dancing, held on the Thursday before Jesus' crucifixion on Good Friday and it honors the spiritual trial of Christ as he prayed in the garden of Gethsemane, when he is supposed to have asked that "this cup be removed from me," that his destiny to die by crucifixion be lifted. But then came his complete surrender, in the prayer: "Thy will, not mine, be done."

All night, as I enter Jesus' plight in Gethsemane, I am aware that surrendering my personal will is my destiny as well. But I equate surrender of my will with physical death and the thought of dying terrifies me. I go through many of the stages of dying, first denying to myself how terrible I feel and then getting very angry because it seems that death is coming—so soon, way too soon. I want to run away, to get as far away as I can from this church. The *Daime* now tastes utterly foul to me and I don't trust these fanatical Brazilians who keep telling me to be calm when my whole body is shaking with terror. I know the *Daime* is a purgative, but I can't believe how much I vomit. I feel terribly, deathly sick and I'm seething inside. Then I start bargaining. If only I can survive this night, I will do whatever God asks me to do... tomorrow.

I go in and out of being convinced that I will not physically survive. Then I become depressed. But I never go the whole way into acceptance or surrender. I get to see in this work just how far I am from "Thy will, not mine, be done."

Of course I do survive physically, but in the morning, when we climb into an open-backed pickup truck to be driven to our *pousada*, I am completely exhausted—and pretty sure I will never again drink that foul, life-threatening, sickening, obnoxious, gooey tea. I can hardly believe it when my friend and Pam's godfather, John, speaks up cheerily during our bumpy ride home: "Isn't this the greatest thing ever?" I think he must have lost his mind.

❧

I do drink *Daime* again. Over the next year we make several more extended visits to this community in Mauá. We are so grateful for the serendipity of having been offered work teaching in Brazil, which allows us to afford to come to Mauá so frequently. Sometimes we come separately, but when Donovan and I both come, Pam travels with us, and she stays with friends in the community while we participate in the ceremonies.

I continue, however, to have a very difficult time in the works. I throw up deeply and often. The words of some of the hymns seem judgmental and moralistic to me, and I respond by judging these hymns. I argue with the words; I dislike aspects of the "doctrine" of the church; I resist being part of an organized religion. My resistance to surrendering to the form of the ceremonies just makes me vomit all the more. I do discover, however, that each time I purge, I feel more of the chronic anxiety and fear held in my body being released.

In spite of my difficulties and resistance, I continue with the ceremonies because I do trust the *Daime* as a teacher (even though I question some of the beliefs and forms of the church that has grown up around it) and because Donovan is so sure this is his path now. I trust him to help me find my way to what he has found here.

My perseverance is rewarded. In the works I am visited more and more by the archetype of the Divine Mother. To be in the presence of pure, complete, unconditional love is deeply healing. And deeply surprising. The love that emanates from this feminine presence I sense —or sometimes see in visions—is of an entirely different order and nature than human love. Human love, coming through the vehicle of our ordinary consciousness, is limited, usually conditional, and always temporary. People love, but just sometimes—when they aren't too tired or feeling aggrieved or preoccupied with getting the next meal. People don't love fully, unconditionally, without end. But divine love is eternal, always present, and does not depend on circumstances or conditions. It blows my mind to be in the presence of this love, knowing that I need do nothing to deserve it.

I learn to open my heart wide so I can receive this presence. As a woman who felt I had not received sufficient nurturing from my biological mother, I now realize that this is the love I have always craved. I am so amazed and grateful that what my whole being needs is now being showered upon me. My belief in having been deprived of affection is gradually being lifted. It becomes clear that underneath my story of insufficient mothering is this vast field of unconditional love. In reality, I lack nothing.

I find that, whether or not I am in ceremony, when I pray to the Divine Mother, simply saying "Mother, I am with you"—or the more traditional "Holy Mary, Mother of God, pray for us now and at the hour of our death"—my body relaxes, my mind becomes still, and I receive Her unconditional love. It becomes a daily source of inner nourishment, especially gratifying whenever I find myself flooded with anxiety.

I spend time every day communing with the Mother. I am especially drawn to being alone in nature. Finding such deep comfort through opening to the Source of unconditional, universal love, I can see why people leave their families and go into convents and monasteries so as not to be distracted from ongoing contact with this nourishing presence. At these moments, I really feel that I don't need or want any more human drama in my life.

But life has other plans for me. The spiritual rubber is about to meet the rocky road of my life with my daughter.

After nearly a year of our drinking *Daime*—in December 1993—during my third extended visit to Brazil, Donovan and I receive shocking news. I have been deeply enjoying myself during a ceremony in which I've been in ecstatic union with the Divine Mother. José meets us at the door of the church and demands that we talk to him, immediately. Donovan and I walk with him to the community office and he tells us that, while we have been singing and dancing all day in church, Pam has had sex with a teenage boy from outside the community. José explains that she had gone to a nearby waterfall with other kids her age where she had met and flirted with this boy who then teased and pressured her into submitting to him sexually. She didn't seem to know she could say no.

In an attempt to avoid a repeat of this event, Donovan and I had decided not to bring Pam back to the *Daime* community during the following year—only to have something much worse happen right near our home in Virginia.

From this time on I am plunged deeply into the human drama of my story with my daughter.

CHAPTER 5

God Is Real and Inside Me

Mauá, Brazil, April 1995

SINCE Pam's sexual encounter in Brazil and her rape in Virginia we have been deeply puzzled about how to help our daughter. Now, as we are on our way back to Brazil to get help for ourselves, Pam is asking to drink *Daime* with us. Could this be the help we've been looking for?

In Rio we board a bus to the interior of Brazil, and then, four hours later, our bus bounces over the Mantiqueira mountains on an unpaved road. Finally we descend down the steep and winding slopes into the small town of Visconde de Mauá. The final stage of the journey is an eight-mile cab ride in a tiny VW bug on a dirt road with car-sized potholes to the *Daime* community called Céu da Montanha (Mountain Heaven), located in the southern end of the always-green Mauá Valley.

We take our question about Pam to José. As psychiatrist, José spends time evaluating and counseling her, and he tells us he thinks she can handle the sacrament. As spiritual leader, José affirms that he will accept her into the ceremonies.

As the time approaches for a scheduled work, Pam calmly reaffirms, "I'm ready to drink *Daime*." I know that both Donovan and José have great faith in the *Daime* as a way to help Pam.

I'm much less sure. "What if she needs someone to be with her?" I ask José. He suggests that I make it my job to be with Pam during the work. I'm relieved; that way I can keep close track of her. As in all

Daime works, everyone present drinks the sacrament, but José assures me that he will give me a little less than usual so I can make Pam my primary focus.

The work is held in the large, round (hexagonal) communal church. Men and women are on opposite sides of the church, surrounding the six-sided, star-shaped altar in the middle, at the center of which is a pole with two cross-pieces on which the *ayahuasca* jungle vine grows. We will sing hymns and dance prescribed steps all night along.

As the work begins, I feel very calm. I realize with gratitude that I have been beautifully prepared in earlier *Daime* works for this specific task. I have already received many lessons about letting go of my self-will as a mother and, instead, trusting the Divine Mother to guide my interactions with Pam. As the work starts, I inwardly keep my attention on the Mother, calmly, completely centered in Her. At one point, the Mother's presence is so intense I see silver-blue sparkles everywhere. Pam is dancing in a different section of the church, where the young women dance.

She comes over and asks me to go with her into the back room which is set aside for those in need of healing. She starts crying uncontrollably. I hold and soothe her and reassure her that it's okay to let go. When she can get words out, she says, "There've been so many times (since the rape) when I felt like crying, but I haven't because it isn't cool."

A little later, she asks plaintively, "The *Daime* is supposed to be teaching me things. What is it teaching me?" I suggest the *Daime* is like a truth serum and it is showing her the truth of her feelings. It is teaching her to let go of the mask, the pretense of coolness.

Her body is leaning into mine, and she is very reluctant to let me go when I need to leave for the bathroom. I return in just a few minutes, but I can see that the time away has impacted her deeply. She half-sobs, "I missed you. I need you. I was so upset when you weren't here." I hold her close. She is so vulnerable, so young, fully feeling her profound infantile need for her mother. She continues to cry, bringing up things about her past, including the poignant lament: "I never was a child."

My heart hurts for her. I feel for that four-year-old who had an adult man's sexual energy thrust upon her and I cry with her for her lost innocence. I feel also for the traumatized infant she was, unable to rest in a secure bond with her biological mother. I sense the terrible lack of safety in her very early life.

Then comes another flood of her tears as she pours out her ambivalence about becoming a grownup. "I don't feel ready to grow up. I feel safest when I'm with you and Dad." At this moment I feel deeply bonded with her. I impress on myself the fact that even when she appears to be rejecting me, she's not really. This deep need is always underneath.

Then she goes into a very scary place, feeling she can't breathe. She says her chest is very tight, constricted. I remind her to pay attention to the fact that she is breathing. "Your body gets tense when it's scared," I tell her. "But you don't need to be afraid of the fear. Just accept that you're afraid and notice that you're still breathing."

She relaxes a little and her breathing naturally deepens. "So," she asks, "when I feel like I can't breathe, it means I'm scared and I need to calm down."

"Yes," I confirm.

Then she begins a more bizarre journey. She feels her hand detaching from her body, as though it doesn't belong to her. Then this feeling of dissociation spreads to more of her body. "I feel like there's a spirit inside my body—and really, the body belongs to it, not to me." I suggest she try to make contact with this spirit, to see what it is and what it wants. She can't manage to do this, but the idea is planted. It's clear to me that she's being taken to another level of her being.

At last she comes back to normal bodily sensation, and we go into the church where everyone is still singing and dancing. I leave her in the care of some young women—guardians of the work—and go to my assigned place to dance.

A few minutes later I look over and see that Pam's face is ashen. Then her body goes slack and slumps to the floor. I inhale deeply and remind myself that I have seen this before in *Daime* works. I quickly thread through the aisles of women to return to Pam's side. I get a little nervous when one of the guardians starts feeling her pulse, but I hold her head and talk to her for the full three minutes it takes for her to come back. When Pam regains consciousness, she says she feels much better.

She begins dancing and singing the hymns which are, of course, in Portuguese. It isn't easy to sing in a foreign language, much less dance while singing, the very first time one takes the sacrament. Pam has truly given herself over to maintaining the form of this *Daime* ceremony.[2] And that affects me. The rigid band that has constricted my heart since the rape is finally relaxing. At this moment my heart is fully open to Pam. I'm touched by her realness, her love, and her courage.

Pam sings with us until the mid-work *intervalo* (intermission). She then describes to me her fainting experience. Aware of slumping onto the floor, she then felt lifted up and out of her body, seeing it from above. Her resting body was enveloped in red-brown clouds of sparkling, lively energy with a blue dolphin leaping out of the red clouds.

Then, just as suddenly as she had left it, she returned to awareness of her body from the inside. She said that when she emerged from the faint, she felt cleansed and very strong physically, able and willing to rejoin the singing and dancing.

---

[2]The *Santo Daime* church ceremonies always include singing songs, called hymns, which are believed to be channeled from the spirit world. The teachings of the religion are contained in the hymns. The singing of hymns comes from the ancient tradition followed in indigenous Amazonian *ayahuasca* rituals which always include songs, called *icaros*, sung by the leader, a shaman who "hears" these songs from the spirit of *ayahuasca*. In the *Santo Daime* church everyone sings the hymns, and anyone may receive a hymn, though typically only those received by the founders of the church are sung on a regular basis.

After the *intervalo* Pam goes to the children's area to rest, and she sleeps for most of the second half of the work, coming back at the end to sing and dance the closing hymns. I'm so impressed with her effort.

While Pam is resting, I am filled with gratitude to the Mother, who had so gloriously been in charge of Pam's work and whose calmness and love I was able to radiate to Pam. I am swimming in a sweet cozy ocean of divine love. I feel this love so deep in my cells that I believe I can never again forget that I am Her beloved daughter, entirely and forever safe. My singing and dancing are effortless.

I vow an even deeper level of surrender: I am willing to let go of whatever in my personality and lifestyle needs to be released. I find I am repeating a line from one of the hymns: *"Eu digo sim, eu digo tá"* (*I say yes, I say yes*). Yes, I surrender fully to you, my Mother, my Master, my guide."

At the end of the work, José joins the two of us and says to Pam, "Your healing has begun." Donovan joins us and says, "I'm so proud of you, Pam."

Hearing the story of her work, José reminds us of the archetypal shamanic healing experience of "dismemberment" in which the patient is taken out of the body and into the spirit realms, where the body is taken apart so it can be reconfigured in a healthier form. He suggests that the *Daime* has taken a strong interest in Pamela and her healing. José feels that the blue dolphin symbolizes Pam's spirit leaping free of the red-brown clouds of her body's traumas.

After the work, Pam is quieter, more introspective than I have ever seen her. She says she knows now that the *Daime* is something real, not just her parents' "airy-fairy" New Age pastime.

In Pam's words:
My parents and the other grownups would go to this church and I didn't really understand it. They would come out talking about throwing up and other funny things. But they would be

glowing.

I decide I want to do it. So I have this long talk with the leader of the church, José Rosa.

The first time I go to a ceremony I cry so much. Just cry and cry. For the first time in my life I know that there is something else than just this material world and that I am something else than just this physical body. This realization is a lot for my little mind.

When I was ten I had sworn off God, completely convinced that God did not exist. My first *Daime* ceremony changes everything. Now I know that God is real.

After the rape I felt so ripped apart, so destroyed. I thought that I would never heal. I know now that I will. The *Daime* shows me that my sickness is not who I am, it is just the part of me that needs healing.

ꙅ

A few nights later, Pamela reports a dream: She is one of twins who remain invisible to each other unless they are both in the same room at the same time. (Her astrological sign is Gemini.) The two girls meet in a room. Pam (the twin she identifies with) is terrified of this other girl and quickly runs away into another room. There she crouches into a fetal position, where she remains as the dream ends. She wakes up frightened but later reflects, "I know there are two sides of me—the good side and the bad side—and I don't know how to get them together."

Gamely, Pamela is enthusiastic about trying another *Daime* ceremony. This one is held outside, and we are encouraged to walk around in nature. She takes my hand and shows me a large, glowing, peach-colored hibiscus flower. "Look, Mom, can you see the fairies dancing in the center of the flower?" I peer deep into the maroon and white heart of the flower. "It looks like a great fairy house to me!" We both giggle. She again seems so young, so open to innocence and wonder, something I haven't seen in her for years.

The final ceremony is held in a large communal meeting room. A dozen of us are invited to lie down and simply receive the spiritual energies being generated by those who are singing hymns to us and praying for us. José directs the work.

Pam was always a nervous and restless child. She couldn't maintain eye contact or sit still. Her agitation has increased dramatically after her recent rape trauma. During this work, however, she lies completely still, emanating a peacefulness I have never seen in her. She seems to be going deep inside herself. Donovan arises from where he was lying on the floor and goes to Pamela. He hears an inner voice telling him to place his hands on her head, and he is told that this action is aiding some rewiring of her brain that is going on. Pam receives his attention with gratitude, an attribute that has been completely lacking lately.

At the conclusion of the ceremony, Pam rises and quietly says, "Now I know that God is inside me. I know I can be healed. I belong here. This is my place."

Then she gets up and goes to the communal kitchen to help prepare the midday meal, moving with complete poise and self-possession. I've never seen her like this, nor ever heard her speak in this manner. There is no trace of the usual adolescent rebellion. She seems grounded, serious, energized and ready to help out. After working in the kitchen, she goes to visit some community members who have a new baby. She voluntarily goes to the evening prayer meeting at the church. For me, Pam's demeanor during and after this ceremony feels like a miracle, after all she has been through during the previous months. I am speechless with gratitude.

José suggests that after Pam's school lets out in June, we take a year off from teaching at Sevenoaks and come to this community to live. Pam thinks this would be great, but her enthusiasm might have to do with the fact that there is no school in Mauá. We are certain that she needs to continue her education.

As we leave Mauá, the site of Pam's remarkable awakening to God, we are unsure what we will do next.

CHAPTER 6

Run to the Slums

Salvador, Bahia, Brazil, July – December 1995

WE all agree that a year in Brazil sounds like the right next step for our family. Being thrown together to explore a new country sounds like fun, and accessibility to the *Daime* now seems essential for our healing as a family.

But Donovan and I are clear that we don't want to live in the Mauá *Daime* community. We are daunted by the primitive conditions: the church is served by outhouses, the only housing available for us is not much more than a shack, the communal dining room is small and unsanitary, and there are no telephones and only erratic electricity.[1] We also realize that we are not ready to submit to José's leadership. These are all deterrents, but the most significant obstacle is the lack of schooling for Pam.

We are drawn instead to the beautiful colonial city on the northeast coast of Brazil—Salvador, Bahia—where we have been teaching Pathwork for the last few years. Donovan would have plenty of work and I could stay home with Pam. We could all attend weekend *Daime* works led by a Brazilian anthropologist who is becoming a friend.

---

[1]Visiting the *Santo Daime* community in Mauá now is much easier and more comfortable. There are phones and electricity, new bathrooms at the church, a new spacious and sanitary dining area, and adequate guest housing. Recently, the road to Mauá has been paved.

We would not have the intense pressure of living day to day in a church community, and we could sidestep the issues we have with José's exercise of his authority. We could regroup as a nuclear family and live by the ocean. Most important, Pamela could attend a good Pan-American bi-lingual school there. Though we want to pursue the *Daime* path, we also want to maintain our middle-class lifestyle.

So it's decided. We'll spend our sabbatical year in Salvador.

✺

We rent an apartment in a condominium just across the road from the ocean. For the first two months, it feels like heaven.

Every morning after Pam gets on the bus to school, I walk the beach welcoming the new day. I watch fishermen tend their nets, and meditate while sitting on rocks at the ocean's edge. My eyes relax and receive the blue, white, and tan meeting of surf and sand... my ears fill with the sound of waves tumbling onto shore. Like an infant reassured by being held close to her mother's beating heart, the rhythmic crashing of waves reminds me that I am being held by a larger comforting maternal presence. Slowly the troubles created by my mind's worry thoughts melt away in the presence of this vastness. On occasion my mind completely gives way, surrendering into the oceanic spaciousness beyond thought. In those blessed seconds of relief from worry, I am reminded: all is well, there is nothing to fear.

Every evening when he's not teaching in Salvador, São Paulo, or elsewhere in Brazil, Donovan joins me lounging in beach chairs oceanside, watching the waves, sipping from fresh coconuts, and enjoying the sunset. My mind and body are slowly healing from the traumas of the last six months.

I look forward to joining the town's inhabitants in celebrating the feast day of Yemanjá, the West African goddess of the oceans, who arrived on these shores with the slaves centuries ago and is still worshipped throughout Brazil. In Salvador statues of Yemanjá are almost as prevalent as statues of Mary, including prominent displays in banks and public buildings. On February 2 many Baianas will turn out for a ritual at *Rio Vermelho* beach—carrying a statue of the Goddess, lighting candles, putting offerings into baskets and sending them out to sea in boats.

We spend every weekend together as a family exploring our surroundings—taking boat trips to the bay islands, driving up the coast to a preserve for sea turtles, and traveling inland to another old colonial town. Most weekends, we go to a *Daime* ceremony with our anthropologist friend Dr. Edward McRae, a Scottish-Brazilian who teaches at a university in Salvador and has studied and written extensively about the *Santo Daime*. I enjoy drinking *Daime* with Edward and his anthropologist friends. They are not "true believers," and have a healthy detachment from the belief system of this church. At the same time, they are committed to experiencing firsthand what they are studying.

We talk for hours about the *Daime*, trying to understand this magical drink and its use, both in the context of contemporary Brazilian religions and in its original shamanic setting. Edward is very kind to Pam and enjoys her company, but Pam is much more resistant to drinking *Daime* with Edward than she was with José. In one work, she spends most of the time throwing up. Thereafter she often refuses the sacrament, or takes only a little.

Donovan and I explore other expressions of Afro-Brazilian spirituality in Salvador. We attend some *Candomblé* ceremonies. During the rituals—derived from West Africa—participants dress in white and move hypnotically to the beating of drums, going into trance, incorporating spirit entities and then offering healings to others.

We also attend ceremonies of the *União do Vegetal* (UDV), the other Brazilian church that uses *ayahuasca* as its sacrament. We even attend a *feitio* (a ritual in which the *ayahuasca* tea is made) with members of this church, including the famous Jamaican singer Jimmy Cliff.

Pam is thrilled to meet Jimmy Cliff, but she won't drink the sacrament at the UDV ceremonies. Still, she behaves herself while we are there.

I work hard to learn Portuguese as few people speak English in Salvador. Every shopping trip is an adventure. At the old-fashioned hardware store where one orders goods at a counter, I tentatively ask for the paint I want. Will I get blue paint (*tinta azul*) or will I be given bathroom tiles (*azulejos*)?

❧

Unlike her parents, Pam learns Portuguese quickly, and is fluent several months after school starts. She tells us that school is okay, and I spend time every afternoon helping her with homework. We get her a math tutor, since that is always her weakest subject. Her writing teacher has taken quite an interest in Pam, and shares with us one of Pam's essays:

> *Who am I? My friends call me crazy. My mom calls me Pam. And I call myself so many things I couldn't write them on five hundred pieces of paper. I have seen so much, and it is all so confusing. Sometimes I want to do something just because it's strange or different, usually dangerous. People don't know me. I don't love or hate getting hurt. It's just part of my life. I think I'm numb. I can't conclude who I am, because I'm not dead ... yet.*

While Donovan and I find the content of the essay alarming, at least Pam is writing and talking out her feelings with this teacher, who is becoming her trusted confidant. We hope that some healing is taking place.

After school, when her homework is complete, Pam is out on the beach or in other apartments in the condominium with her friends. She stops talking to us. I feel sympathetic to immigrant parents in the

U.S. who have to watch helplessly as their children learn English and become swallowed up in an American culture they do not approve of and cannot navigate.

We begin to suspect she is getting into trouble, but we never catch her. We require her to report back to us at our apartment every hour, sometimes every half hour. She complies, but nevertheless, we can feel her rapidly slipping away from emotional connection to us.

Our neighbor Angela comes over one day to tell us that people are talking about Pam. They say she is behaving very badly, using lots of cocaine, and sleeping with a lot of boys. I don't know (or don't want to know) if this is true, or if it's just gossip and prejudice against Americans. If it's true, we're stumped. We're already checking up on her daily at school and having her show up at our apartment every hour after school. She's earning passing grades. I can't imagine what more we can do… so I do nothing.

One Saturday night, Pam goes with the teenage daughter of one of our friends to an outdoor rock concert. We are startled when the girl's mother shows up at our door late that night with a drunken Pam. The next day Pam relates, "I drank a lot of beer. Everything was fuzzy and I wasn't sure where I was. I figured that what I needed to get straight was just to drink another beer, so I kept drinking." I can't imagine how her thinking can be so insane.

In November, Donovan has to go back to the U.S. for a week to work. While he's away, Pam starts demanding more time outside with her friends and is surly or overtly hostile every time she talks to me. One night she insists on going out after ten p.m. When I say no, she heads for the door anyway. I stand between her and the door, and we start a shoving match. A part of me is horrified at what I'm doing—how could I have descended into such madness with her? I get confused, my grip on her wrist slips, and she ducks under my arms and out the door.

I call my friend Edward to ask what he thinks I should do. He suggests it's probably just typical adolescent behavior. I know it isn't, but I want to believe him. Pam stays out until two a.m. She comes back subdued and apologetic, and tells me she just went to the beach, alone, to think about her life. Not knowing what else to do, I believe her.

❧

In December, almost exactly a year after being raped, Pamela disappears from our condominium. It is the eve of the feast day of *Nossa Senhora da Conceição* (Our Lady of Conception), a school holiday. She calls that evening to say she is safe and staying with her boyfriend Ricardo. We have never met him. She tells me she will come back in the morning.

But she does not return, nor does she call. That evening I have my first full-fledged panic attack. My body flails on the bed; my breathing is rapid, intense, and shallow, and my heart is racing. I try to take a deep breath and cannot. Donovan is by my side, emanating a calmness that comes from a deep well inside. I can recognize it in him, but I cannot follow him there. He holds my hands, strokes my face, and murmurs reassuring words. He prays and sings hymns to me. Nothing gets through; I am inconsolable. I wail and thrash about on the bed until, finally, the panic subsides and I can speak again.

I realize, as I watch all the horrible scenarios swirling in my head, that I'm not just afraid for Pam and for her future—I'm also afraid for myself. I still hold tightly to an image of myself as a loving and caring mother. Pam's behavior threatens to destroy this image. Could I live with myself if we lost her to the streets of Salvador? Could I endure the judgments of others about letting my daughter run loose in such a dangerous place? My mask of goodness and my illusion of control—central to my ideas about who I am—are mortally threatened.

Donovan and I talk about our options. Edward and our other English-speaking Brazilian friends are out of town for the holiday weekend. Our Portuguese is limited. We might try going to the police; if we brought a photo of Pam and offered money, maybe someone would help us look for her. After all, a very white-skinned, blue-eyed girl with light brown hair would stand out anywhere in Salvador. Still, we think it's unlikely we could get much help. We decide to talk to our neighbor Angela in the morning.

The next day I ask Angela in my halting Portuguese if she can have her son Marco try to find out what has happened. Angela comes over a few hours later with her minister to pray over me. Then her son comes back with the report that Ricardo is a part-time surfer and full-time cocaine dealer with a very bad reputation. He is known to force girls to submit to him sexually, and he is known to carry a knife. Ricardo lives in a nearby *favela* (slum) but hangs out in our condominium, at the apartment of an older gay man who lets teenage male dealers use his place. Marco has heard that Ricardo and his friends were planning to go to Arembepe beach that weekend, famous both for surfing and for drug use.

Pam writes:

Stepping off the bus with Ricardo, I walk into a different world, one I do not know. We are in a *favela*. The gutters are filled with rotted food, cigarette butts, and broken toys, all jumbled together. A ghastly smell sears my nose. I grab Ricardo's hand. Small children stare up at me through strands of dirty hair. A dog, no meat on his bones, jumps around a garbage dump.

We head down a flight of busted-up stairs, passing half-built houses with no doors. Inside are dreary faces cast down, bodies sunken into musty couches. We come to a small wooden door with an advertisement for beer on it. I step through into a dark, dusty interior. Ricardo's mother, a large woman, sits at a small table drinking beer. There are already a lot of empty bottles lying on the floor. She looks up at Ricardo with a sad expression on her dirt-stained face. "You got a *gringa* this time," she says, then turns back to her beer.

Ricardo takes me to his room, which consists of one bed and a small table. A light bulb hangs from the ceiling but isn't on because large openings in the wall let in plenty of light. I ask if I can take a shower; the day has been long and the things I've seen are heavy. This is a place I never knew, when I lived in a world where I had plenty to eat and a clean bed and loving parents.

Ricardo shows me the shower, a metal pipe coming out of the wall. He leaves to get me some clean clothes. After my shower, I go to Ricardo's room and fall into bed exhausted.

When I wake up, he brings me some beer. We head out for the streets. I see a child asleep at the bottom of some stairs; at least I hope she's asleep. We pass through a metal door and climb a flight of stairs to a bar on a roof. The lights make me dizzy and my cigarette droops from my hand. The boys drink and discuss their drug deals; I just drink.

Back in the streets, the lights are swirling, my mind is fuzzy. I hear catcalls as Ricardo's "friends" slap him high-fives as we pass. Suddenly, Ricardo slips into an alley and I follow, then stop, startled. Another boy pulls me to him, grabbing, forcing; I don't struggle. Two other boys appear.

Dimly, I'm beginning to feel that Ricardo doesn't want me as his girlfriend; I'm just his toy. I don't care. He's not even that good-looking. But from the first moment I met Ricardo, when he came up to me in the condominium and started kissing me, I knew I would do whatever he wanted.

We all go back to Ricardo's and spend the night with cocaine, beer, and messing around. I'm so fucked up I hardly notice when they start to slap my face and legs; all I remember is their mean laughter and my going far, far away.

When I wake up the next morning I am tangled in a blanket, which feels like a cocoon. The floor is covered with ants and littered with beer bottles. My whole body is shaking. Ricardo hands me a glass of beer, which I gulp down. Then I notice the pain. I look down and see bruises on my legs. I touch my swollen mouth. Ricardo shakes his head, "*Gringa*, go home. The *favelas* are not for you." This I know, but instead I say, "No, let me go with you to the beach."

Ricardo and I, plus three of his friends, take several buses to get to a beach, and we spread out a sheet on the sand where all five of us sleep. I drink every night and snort a lot of cocaine. I eat only rice and tomato paste. I cook on a campfire and wash our only dish and all our clothes in the ocean, with shampoo.

🔖

Donovan and I talk again about what to do. If we drive to the beach, she might bolt and run from us. We know we can't physically catch her if she does, and we don't want to risk her running farther. We know Ricardo is dangerous, and we don't want to threaten him— that might result in more harm to Pam. We keep arriving at the same conclusion: All we can do is wait until the weekend is over and see if Pam returns.

All weekend I am haunted by the memory of a bizarre *miração* (vision) from about a year earlier. After leading a week-long training in Salvador, I attended a *Daime* ceremony in which I was taken high into an astral realm where I witnessed a fierce battle between the forces of darkness and the angels of light. I saw two columns of power: the evil one looked like a tornado of swirling, shadowy forms perpetrating horrendous acts of cutting and brutality; the good one was filled with bright bursts of lightning and angelic forms.

I was carried to the top of the column of light and goodness and told I would need to confront the evil forces. Feeling entirely inadequate to the task, I called on the light of Christ for help. I was told to contact the Christ light within my being and let it radiate the needed power. I wavered, flailing in a self-conscious belief in my weakness, then fell to the bottom of the column of light. At the time, I was told that my failure was only temporary.

I was also shown that this vision of fighting evil was taking place in the city of Salvador, but at that time it made no sense to my rational mind. I thought only of our students there, all of whom were competent, middle-aged professionals, mostly women and trained therapists, who would never act out the kind of evil I was being shown in this *miração*.

Now, as I pray for Pam to return safely, I am jolted by the recognition that this was the *Daime's* foreshadowing of the evil we are now facing in the form of Ricardo. Pam would later tell us Ricardo bragged that he forced young girls in the *favela* to submit to him sexually, scratching them with his knife if they resisted, drawing blood until they were terrified enough to do whatever he wanted.

I begin to see how terribly naïve I am about evil. A central teaching of the Pathwork is the need to face our shadow side, to take responsibility for our personal evil and to see our negativity as a defense against pain. We have helped hundreds of people to understand how they have closed their hearts to themselves and others, to acknowledge their meanness and unconscious cruelty, and then to open their hearts by feeling the personal pain they have been defending against. We have provided a compassionate environment for many people to transform their negativity. Donovan even put together a book of Pathwork teachings entitled *Fear No Evil*. So I thought we were experts.

But now, when evil is hitting so close to home in my own life, all I want is to run away. I can't open my heart enough to accept that this terrible man has a strong grip on my own daughter and is pulling her down into his darkness. I just want it not to be true.

In the years to come my heart would be ripped open many times until I slowly learned to accept all the desperate characters, all the crazy acting-out, and all the pain that the disease of addiction would bring into our lives. Ultimately, my mind would be stopped cold. I would give up the idea that I knew anything at all about evil, realizing instead that my mind's effort to hold on to explanations and causes was just another defense against the raw reality of simple, heartbreaking pain.

§⋒

At the end of the weekend Pam comes back home—badly sun-burned, wild-eyed, and defiant. In her words: "My back was blistering. I was like dead. I was so lost. It was the best time I had ever had."

When she is with us again, my relief and anger are so tangled up I don't know what to say to her. She sits on the couch and we ask her questions, most of which she won't answer. She keeps saying, "I'm okay. I'm sorry you're upset, but that's really not my problem. Just get over it."

I am impressed by her self-confidence and say to Donovan, "Maybe we just need to trust her." He is shocked at my naiveté, seeing more clearly than I do that Pamela is completely out of control, at fourteen years of age.

Pam insists on going out again, saying she will check in every hour. Donovan is opposed to letting her out of our sight, but I am still in shock and so I accede to her request. I'm both intimidated by her bravado and oddly awed by the boldness that enabled her to survive the *favela*. I know very little about the disease of addiction that has already taken hold of her. I'm seeing through the rose-colored glasses of my own denial, made up partly of ignorance and partly of my own emotional dependency. This blurred vision leads me to placate her in a crazy, desperate effort to maintain connection with her at any price.

She leaves our apartment.

Donovan says he feels the bottom dropping out of his stomach. He's known for a long time that Pamela is crazy, but now he feels that I've gone crazy too. Maybe he is the only sane one among us. He has the sickening feeling that now he is alone with the problems of Pam's insanity—and mine.

Donovan insists, "We all need to get out of Salvador, immediately." He's relieved when I agree. We had been planning to go to Mauá for Pam's school's Christmas break. Now we know we have to go *now*—and not tell Pam we are never coming back. We call the airlines and book a flight for the next day. All we have to do is get Pam back before then.

She doesn't return when she said she would, so we go looking for her. We ask the young people around the complex to tell us where she is. They direct us to an apartment building where they last saw her. She comes out a few minutes later and Donovan grabs her arm, leading her forcefully back to our apartment. When we get there, she says, "I don't have to stay here if I don't want to." She threatens to push past Donovan; he pushes her back against a wall and tells her he will not let her leave again. Pam whines about his rough treatment.

I feel awful. I'm torn between the two people I love most in the world. I don't trust her, and I don't trust him. I'm afraid his forcefulness will alienate her further. But I also don't trust myself. I am floundering, adrift, without an emotional or spiritual center.

The next day in the Salvador airport, as we wait for our flight to Rio, Pam says she feels sick. I accompany her to a small, empty emergency health clinic where she lies down on a gurney. I don't realize that she's suffering from alcohol and cocaine withdrawal. In fact, she's been drinking and using cocaine for months now, which is why her *Daime* works have been mostly purgative. This was the *Daime's* way of trying to clean her body of the poisons she'd ingested.

We land in Rio, wrestle our baggage into a taxi, and ride to the big central bus terminal where we board a bus for the interior. At the small city of Resende, we change to another bus for Mauá. Through all these changes, we are afraid Pam might bolt from us. When we get settled on the bus to Mauá, we breathe a sigh of relief.

Now we know that we have to drop the pretense of living a normal middle-class life—and find some way to heal our family.

CHAPTER 7

No Escape from Ourselves

Mauá, Brazil, December 1995 – April 1996

WE arrive in the *Santo Daime* community and go directly to José's house. He embraces us and says, "I'm glad you're home." I weep.

Others in the community also welcome us. An aspect of the church that has always touched me deeply is how it opens its doors to all people. The church is a haven for many poor people, both in the Amazon and from Brazilian cities. Many social rejects, such as drug addicts seeking recovery and street people seeking respite, are welcomed into this church. The *Santo Daime* is active in its mission to help both the poor and the psychically wounded.

At this moment, I feel like one of society's outcasts myself.

José has just started a program for two other young people (one American and one Brazilian) with addiction problems, so Pam has a context for her healing. José puts her on a special detox diet to clear the cocaine from her system and assigns two stable young women in the community to be with her; he calls them her *"amigas qualificadas"* (qualified friends[1]). One of them will accompany her at all times when she is not with us. Pam agrees to participate in the program and seems visibly relieved to be back in Mauá, where she feels she belongs.

---

[1]Meaning that these young women were qualified to be Pam's true friends.

Donovan and I are willing to shed our conventional ideas and our personal preferences about how we want to live. We are finally desperate enough, humble enough, and brave enough to let go of how we've wanted our lives to be, and instead accept where life has led us. We purchase the little wooden house we had rejected before as a shack, and we hire a carpenter to start repairs.

As resistant as I still sometimes feel to José's command of the community, I am very grateful for his willingness to accept our family and take Pam under his wing. He talks with us about his vision for creating a holistic healing center here, which would include massage, hydrotherapy, psychological work, energetic healing, and more, along with the *Daime* ceremonies. He envisions attracting people from the Brazilian cities of Rio de Janeiro and São Paulo, as well as Americans and Europeans who want to experience the *Daime* in a setting less foreign than deep in the Amazon. He has ambitious plans to upgrade the facilities and sponsor a variety of workshops. Donovan and I have twenty years of practical experience in creating and leading a center for personal transformation, and this answers José's need for help in manifesting his vision. He's certain that we are supposed to be here, helping to bring about the evolution of the Mauá community into a healing center.

Battered as I feel, I do not challenge José. Helping him feels like a worthwhile mission, and truly, I don't know what else might be right for us. Our choice of Salvador was disastrous for Pam, and one of the few things that's clear to me is that it was my self-will and pride—my insistence on living a comfortable middle class life—that placed us there. Certainly, living in the Mauá *Daime* community wasn't my plan, but it is, apparently, life's plan for us now.

My spiritual work is to trust where our lives have led us. It is time to get serious about following the *Daime* as our teacher—one who, apparently, has called us to communal life.

❧

Our little wooden house occupies less space than does our living room back in Virginia. The shower (when we have water) is cold. When we have electricity, the refrigerator works only if we kick it hard enough. The two burners on the stove usually function whenever we manage to get a *botijão de gás* (a container of propane gas) hauled from the town of Mauá an hour away. Of the three luxuries of modern life—running water, electricity, and inside heat for cooking—we are lucky if we have two of them operating at the same time.

We share the house with the largest, blackest, hairiest spiders and the most aggressive stinging red ants I have ever seen.

At midday each day, we walk twenty minutes to the center of the community, where we share with others a meal of rice, beans, and vegetables. We go to the large round church at least once a day, sometimes twice, for daily prayer services. Once a week we join in day-long rituals there.

It is another twenty-minute walk plus a twenty-minute bus ride to the town of Mauá where minimal groceries and canisters of stove gas are available. We purchase all our furniture in the small city of Resende, yet another hour away by bus.

The serene beauty of the rolling green hills and the soothing sweetness of ever- blooming jasmine flowers help make the hardships bearable. But of course we have not come for the scenery, but for the power of the spiritual work that is done here. Donovan's dropping his addiction to cigarettes, my opening to the Divine Mother, Pam's brief experience of inner peace—these changes bring hope. As long as there is hope for Pam, we will stay here.

❧

The only person Pam will listen to is José. He becomes her confidant, her psychiatrist, and her spiritual director. Pam adores José and respects his authority in ways that she no longer does ours... or anyone else's. I am able to relinquish to José my usual tense desire to control Pam. I'm so grateful he is ready to take her on, and we are hopeful of real and greater change. José talks to Pam almost every day, and he leads special healing ceremonies for her and the two other young people, sometimes as often as twice a week. Donovan attends every ceremony with Pam and drinks the sacrament whenever she does.

José performs a specific ceremony with Pam to exorcise negative spirits. It's a stretch for us to accept that she might really be possessed, not just by inner psychological demons but by actual entities. José teaches us about *pombas-giras*, spirits that seek negative sexual excitement and attach to people who have been deeply wounded sexually. His theory about spirit possession makes some sense of her bizarre, self-destructive sexual behavior. He addresses these and other dark entities that he "sees" attached to her, and directs them to release their hold on her and go to the light. She says she feels lighter and more herself after these ceremonies.

Pam writes about one of them:

Painful scenes from my time in Salvador flash in my mind. I cry a lot and feel José with me. Lying on a mattress, with my eyes closed, I see dark lights, and red and black beings flying around. I am seeing hell.

I get scared and, in my mind, I ask José to show me something beautiful. As I look, a yellow light appears to cover the darkness, and a pink rose (which I know is José Rosa) blooms before my eyes. José is there in my heart and he shows me that there is a God and he is always with me. He shows me a part of me that can love and trust. I'm scared, so I push that part back. He teaches that you can't live if you don't know how to love.

I do know how, but most of the time I am too scared to trust in myself or in God.

With the help of José's counseling and the *Daime* works, Pam begins to face her fears and, tentatively, reclaim her trust. Under his guidance, she is again opening to the reality of a spiritual higher power.

Many years later Pam would write:

While it took a long time before I could begin to deal with my addictions, my experiences with José and the *Daime* in Mauá sustained me during the darkest days yet to come. I always knew that God was with me, even in my years of craziness and drugs and problems. No matter what. God lives in everyone and it is just a matter of remembering that this is so. As long as I knew God was real and lives in me, I knew hope was real. I knew that nothing (even me) could be hopeless forever. I have known this to be true since the first time I drank *Daime,* when I was thirteen years old.

🔖

Though much of the work with negative spirits seems odd to us, it is undeniable that our daughter is getting better. We sing hymns with her daily. She talks about God; she wants to find inner peace. Right after a ceremony with José, Pam is always saner: more open, honest, and self-respecting. She conscientiously studies the church's many hymns and even memorizes whole hymnbooks. We know this work is good for her, though she is often cold and hostile to us, especially after the effects of her work with José fade.

We know she is constantly tempted to flirt with boys, leave the community, and use drugs, but she stays and does her work.

While I miss the physical comforts of our home in Virginia and our lovely apartment by the ocean in Salvador, I am finding deep spiritual comfort through connection with the Divine Mother in the beautiful countryside of Mauá—especially through the river, replete with waterfalls, that cuts through the valley and flows beside the community.

I am actually enjoying simplifying my life down to the basics. I love the daily long walks to and from the community's dining area and church, listening to frogs at night, and smelling flowers by day. I enjoy spending most of each day focused on the work of simple survival—getting food and maintaining shelter.

My self-will is relaxing as I accept the frustrations and challenges that emerge each day. For a while our water doesn't function, and we have to haul water from the river so we can flush the toilet. We boil river water for bathing, and carry containers of drinking water from the communal kitchen where the water is run through a purifier.

Sometimes I clean the kitchen only to see it overrun an hour later by the ever- present red ants. One day I might plan to work in the office but find the computer is down. The communal kitchen may be understaffed that day, so instead I chop vegetables all morning. I'm learning to flow with the way the day wants to be lived, letting go of my mental attachment to planning. Slowly, I'm also learning how to surrender more fully to the *Daime* during the works, letting myself be carried rather than trying to be in control. Letting go of self-will is my path, my spiritual discipline for now.

✿

Pam stops having her periods, so we assume she is pregnant. We are not happy about this because we know she is so unready to be a mother. But José and Pam are both adamant that she will keep the baby. We begin to fear that her pregnancy might mean we will have to settle in this community indefinitely, since they are willing to accept us and help Pam with raising her baby.

José is not displeased with this development, as he still wants us to help him create a functional, holistic healing center. He knows such an endeavor would require a long-term commitment on our part.

We have a healing work together as a family to seek guidance about Pam, whose pregnancy now seems certain. As the work starts, I feel surprisingly relaxed and calm, readier than I thought I would be to see or hear whatever will come to me. The force of the *Daime* is strong and palpable, a giant green power of the forest sweeping through, a distinct energy next to which my puny preferences seem trivial. The major, undeniable feeling is that Pam is within this power—her pregnancy is held within a larger reality which I cannot oppose. I must adjust to this reality, not attempt to change it. I feel that this power is attentive to Pam and will prepare her to be a mother. It seems clear that she will stay here, have the baby, and become part of this community. She loves it here; she has found her place.

My mind starts wrapping around a story that our living in the Mauá *Daime* community is central to the unfolding of our destiny as a family. I am influenced by José's sense of the mission of the *Daime*, and of Mauá in particular. In many works I sense the *Daime* church as a vehicle for bringing about the second coming of Christ, the awakening of the Christ consciousness within every human heart. At night after works, I feel guided by the moon and by a star that pulsates vibrantly and seems to be calling me. I entertain the belief that this is like the star in Bethlehem, announcing a cosmically significant new birth of Christ consciousness here in Mauá, Brazil.

In several works I strongly sense that events are being orchestrated at a much higher level than our human minds can comprehend. All I need to do is assent to this larger divine design, as there seems to be a rhythm to the unfolding of events. Pam's first sexual encounter, her rape, and her runaway to the *favela* all occurred on sequential Decembers within a week of each other, culminating in this pregnancy and our living here. This impresses me as a remarkable karmic story, as though written by a cosmic novelist. This is the story we are now living, and I need to surrender, to take my place in it.

I so fully believe this story that I don't even bother to take Pam to a doctor to see if she's really pregnant.

❧

After two months of no periods, Pam starts bleeding; we assume she is having a miscarriage. We have just started an all-day ceremony, so José cannot come with us to the hospital. We hire Mark, the other young American here for healing, to drive José's jeep over the dirt mountain road, bumping along for over an hour, to the nearest hospital in Resende. José warns Mark to drive slowly so we don't lose the baby.

Donovan, on the other hand, will confide to me later that "with every jolt of the jeep on the bumpy road, I was praying for the fetus to be jarred loose." Sensing this, Pam is hostile to him.

Pam is given an ultrasound, and we're told to talk to a doctor immediately. The doctor speaks no English, so, with Pam translating, we struggle to understand his report. Pam is not pregnant, probably never has been. Instead, there is an enormous cyst on her right ovary that has caused her periods to stop. It must be removed right away. We want to get José's medical opinion before we agree, but there is no phone in the community so we have no way to contact him. We send Mark back with an urgent message for José to come to Resende. But this will take a day at least, and the doctor tells us there is no time to wait, that he needs to remove the cyst now. And we must pay him $3,000, also *now*. His urgency convinces us, and we find a way to wire money to him. Pam is wheeled in for surgery.

A couple of hours later, the doctor shows up in the waiting room with a glass jar containing a baseball-sized hunk of flesh, which he says is the cyst he has cut out. He tells us he has also removed her right ovary. An hour or so later, Pam is wheeled into a minimally furnished room where we await her. I ask for a mattress so I can stay with her; they can only offer me a chair. As soon as she wakes, she turns her back to me and says, "Leave. I don't want you to stay with me." That's how bad things are between us.

I stay anyway, of course. This turns out to be crucial because the hospital is understaffed and her catheter bottle needs changing more often than the nurses can do it. I nurse her and sit with her all night. In the middle of the night, she bolts upright and blurts out, "I woke up in the middle of the surgery and saw blood everywhere!" She goes on to tell me the surgical staff had quickly given her more anesthesia and she'd gone back to sleep. As I sit with her distress and hear her fear of seeing all that blood, I can tell that, slowly, something is softening in her. She's more civil—actually communicating.

Knowing that Pam isn't pregnant helps Donovan relax. He starts making jokes, to which Pam responds well. We both notice that when his energy shifts, hers does too. By the time José shows up the next morning, we're all joking and having a good time together.

José tells us that ovarian cysts usually don't have to be removed, and that the doctor was probably just looking to make money from Americans. Still, this strange surgery, in this inadequate hospital, has an oddly curative effect. With the removal of her right ovary and cyst, it seems that something terribly negative has been purged from Pam's body, like an exorcism. Her terrible alienation from us, her parents, is lifted—for now.

✺

We have some of our best times together as a family after this. The small house we share, and the need to work together to overcome physical hardships, force a new intimacy that's good for us. The two tiny bedrooms are barely separated by a thin wooden wall; we can hear each other breathe. There is no place for any of us to escape, so we have to deal with our issues more openly than we ever have before.

Pam and I work together to keep our little house swept out and the kitchen clean so we aren't overtaken by ants. We all share in making food in our barely adequate kitchen. Pam and I also work in the communal kitchen sorting beans, chopping vegetables, drying dishes. We work cleaning the church before and after ceremonies. We share the experience of being in ceremony together, singing and dancing to the hymns, and praying in Portuguese, sometimes all night long. Then we make the long walk back to our house, feeling spiritually open and physically tired, stumbling along and laughing together. All of this brings us very close.

So it is with hope for our healing—especially Pamela's—that we stay here, with José helping Pam, and Donovan and I helping José realize his dream of creating a *Santo Daime* center for holistic healing. We struggle through the hardships in the belief that Pam's recovery is underway. She runs away from the *Daime* community a couple of times, but we weather these little storms. It's only a few hours each time and she comes back chastened and ready to try again. We are willing to stay as long as necessary.

❧

Five months after we arrive, Pam runs away with two neighbor boys and spends the night using drugs with them. At the time, I'm in the States doing a workshop I'd contracted to do a year earlier. José is in the hospital for what is assumed to be minor surgery. With both of us gone, Pam seems to lose her bearings.

This time when she runs away, several of the young women complain to José, saying she has gone too far and she's more than they can handle. They don't want to help her anymore; they consider her hopelessly immoral.

The day after Pam has run away, Donovan is in the open area between the church and the dining hall. José's grown stepson comes out of the community office to talk to him, and a small crowd of young Brazilians quickly forms. They are all talking in rapid Portuguese, and it takes Donovan a few minutes to get the message clearly. They are saying, in effect: "José says you have to take Pamela back to the United States *today*. She has to leave here and go back to the U.S. *today*."

It must be that José, still in the hospital, has become convinced that the community can no longer handle Pam. He probably feels he no longer has the help and support he needs to continue being her mentor.

Donovan is stunned by the suddenness of the rejection, especially after hearing so many promises that the community will be there for us as a family. But José is the boss. Since he has made his decision, there is nothing we can do but pack up and leave. Pamela is back in our laps.

Donovan books rooms at a nearby inn and takes Pam there for two days. Then it's a bus to Rio, some shopping for new clothes, and a trip to the airport, where he watches to make sure she gets on the plane. I meet her at the airport in the U.S. while Donovan goes back to Mauá to pack up some of our things. We give our house back to the community, and he gives away most of our belongings.

As Donovan boards the bus again to Rio, he feels acutely his disappointment at the ending of this chapter of our lives. At the same time, he realizes that our time at the Mauá community has brought some real growth. Pam has been clean for almost five months. It certainly helped that we were in a quiet rural environment, far away from the temptations of mass culture. No TV reception and no telephones; life was simple and basic. We lived in a community of people committed to personal growth and contact with God. Pam joined in the community's work and ceremonies and lived very simply, with her parents.

But the two biggest factors that kept her clean for so long were the sacrament of the *Daime* and the presence of unconditional love. The *Daime* was a force she respected. It would have done no good to tell her to trust in a Higher Power. In the works, however, she directly experienced the *Daime* as something bigger, stronger, and wiser than herself, a Higher Power to which she bowed.

And she truly experienced unconditional love, both from Donovan and me and from José, whose authority she respected. Our commitment to Pam was steady at this time, and we maintained our faith—specifically, that she could let the *Daime* in and that the *Daime* could heal her. José had the same faith; he loved Pam and knew that the *Daime* brings in the power of divine love, which can heal anything.

✒

Less than a week after Donovan returns to the States, in April 1996, we receive word that José has suddenly died of complications from surgery. We are shocked, and Pam is devastated. Our dream that this spiritual community would save our daughter is over. Pam is only beginning to heal, and her connection to José has been crucial. His death sends her reeling.

Our hope sputters. We have to admit that the situation we're in with Pam is, once again, more than we can handle. Back in the United States, there are no *Daime* communities and there is no one like José. We know we need to find a new source of help. Soon.

CHAPTER 8

Conscious Deception

New York State, June 1996

I'M in the Charlottesville, Virginia airport waiting for a flight to Elmira, New York, to visit the Chapel School, a therapeutic boarding school for troubled teens. We've decided that this is what Pam needs. She's run away again, this time to the streets of Charlottesville. While Donovan is away teaching in Brazil, I'm going to check out this school to see if it could be the right one for our daughter.

From the noisy airport lobby I make telephone calls to several "transport professionals" recommended by the school. Combining the skills of private detectives and prison guards, these specialists promise that they can find my runaway daughter and take her, by force if necessary, to this school.

An inner alarm goes off even as I lift the receiver to make the call: What kind of place would recommend this dire measure? But I have to admit that it may be necessary, and I would rather have her taken by force to someplace where she can get help rather than let her die on the streets from a drug overdose. By this time, such an outcome is a real, maybe even a likely possibility.

❧

Lying alone on the bed in a nondescript motel room in the bleak and dreary small town close to the school, I feel my clarity and resolve crumble. How will I recognize the right place for Pam? I've already made so many choices for her that haven't worked out well that my self-confidence is shot. Anxious thoughts prick like thorns into raw flesh. I'll have to choose somehow. She's only fifteen; Donovan and I still have to make decisions for her.

I pray for a sign. I'm aware of how desperate I am, and I'm afraid that I'll settle for any place that will take her. Yet I know we need the *right* place, one where Pam's spiritual opening through the *Daime* will be honored while her profound trauma and addictive issues are addressed. I pray again to Mother Mary, a well of boundless love and comfort. The prayer itself becomes my consolation, allowing me to fall, at last, into a fitful sleep.

Arriving at the school the next morning, I can hardly believe my eyes: an almost life-sized ivory-white statue of Mary, hands joined in prayer, greets me on the front lawn of the school. Surely this is my sign. (I later realize that probably every Catholic home and institution in upstate New York has a lawn statue of the Virgin Mary. But in my wounded state, this sign feels like exactly the salve I need.)

I tour the school, which includes plain wooden buildings for classrooms, a crowded dining area, a few cramped staff offices, and trailers for dorms. The only exceptional building is the new chapel, exquisite in every detail, decorated with original paintings, beautiful icons, and fine woodworking. This is clearly a place where the spiritual life takes priority.

But what really seals the decision for me is talking to the girls who show me around. Several have stories that are every bit as bizarre and disturbed as Pam's. Yet these girls are aware and sensitive, candid about their problems, and bubbling and optimistic about their futures. It seems almost too good to be true that my Pam could someday look forward to a bright future the way these girls do.

I have lunch in the school's dining room, which turns out to be a good-bye event for one of the teachers. One by one the students stand to tell their stories and to express their gratitude to this man for helping to save their lives. At several moments most of the faculty and students are crying, and I, too, am moved to tears by what I hear. Spirit is palpably present.

I meet Father Bill, the Catholic priest who helps run the school, managed mostly by Catholic laypeople. Even though I suspect that their conservative politics are far from my own, I'm touched on a spiritual level. I sense a shared knowing that God is the only true healer. And I expect Pam will be open to the Catholic influence as a result of her work in the Brazilian church, which has many Catholic elements. This school is traditional, but it offers regular group therapy and daily Twelve Step work. And it is affordable—barely—costing more like a year at a state college instead of the Ivy League prices most therapeutic boarding schools charge. For once, I feel certain: this is the place for Pam.

I call Donovan in Brazil, and we agree to try to get Pam into the school. We make a plan: I'll fly back tonight so I'll be there in time to receive the call from Pam I expect the next morning. We know she'll never come to the school if I tell her about it, so we decide to make up a story. I'll tell her that she and I are going on a little vacation to visit a friend who lives in upstate New York. Donovan will fly up from Brazil and meet me at the school. His unexpected presence will add to the seriousness of the message we'll be sending her: She needs help and we believe this place can offer it.

With Donovan out of the country I must now be father as well as mother to this child. I feel an influx of courage and firm resolve. I sense that the dormant seeds of inner strength—watered for two years by my drinking *Daime*—are now bursting through the crusty topsoil of my anxious, neurotic personality. No more waffling; no more denial. No more preoccupation with my own thoughts. It's time to act, to do what needs to be done.

My willingness to deceive Pam, even for her own good, is a radical

departure for me. I am always honest, to a fault. I have been especially
scrupulous with my daughter, who has enormous issues with trust.
Normally, I couldn't stand to deceive her consciously.

But this is different: I know her life is at stake. I know that if we
don't get her into a safe place where she can begin to deal with her
self-destructiveness, her addictions will kill her. And though I do not
yet know much about the disease of addiction, I do know that Pam
has entered a place where reason cannot penetrate. Something alien
has grabbed hold of her; she is no longer the daughter who loves me.
She is compelled by something I don't understand. I cannot trust any
promises she might make if I did tell her the truth; in her present state
she would never choose to get help. My determination to save her
from herself has opened up the courage to stand firm, to do what I
could not do in Salvador when she pushed past me and out the door.

I drive to the airport feeling the first glimmer of hope I've had
since leaving Brazil and absorbing the impact of José's death. Now
I pray that I can get her to this school safely. I'm tense, taut with the
seriousness of what I'm facing and what I'll need to do to get her here.
I am on a solemn and important mission.

At the airport ticket counter I'm thrown into turmoil again. I discover that my plane, the last one scheduled to leave today, has been
canceled. There will be no other flight out this night.

"But I have to get home by tomorrow morning," I plead with the
ticket agent. "I have a very sick child at home." He is not moved. Ges-
turing across the terminal with his chin, he suggests I rent a car. Then
he turns and walks away; I'm devastated.

I talk to each of the agents at the few car rental places that are
still open, and I discover that I instantly know who has an open heart
and who does not. At this moment I vow never to close my heart to

anyone in need. Even if I cannot give what a person needs materially, I will always give my compassion. One of the agents hears my story and bends some rules to give me a one-way rental to Charlottesville. I'm so grateful I weep.

And then I make the nine-hour drive, alone, all night, sometimes crying along with country music on the radio. I'm determined to get home in time for the phone call from Pam, and indeed, it comes barely an hour after I return. She wants to stay out another day and then will call me. I entice her with the prospect of a vacation up north. She agrees to have me come pick her up the next morning.

I use the time I have until then to write a biography of her for the school, and pack up some clothes in a large suitcase that I hide in the back of the trunk. In front of it I place the small suitcase we will need for our trip.

The next morning I locate Pam at the apartment complex where she's been staying. She looks awful; her hair has been butchered again. Her clothes are disheveled, and she tells me she's only had sweets to eat for two days; she's starving. She says she's done a lot of cocaine. I don't understand much about cocaine detox, so I just accept it when she needs to sleep a lot that day and is either grouchy or incoherent when she's awake. Somehow, the next day I manage to get us both in the car headed north.

We stop at a Holiday Inn in Pennsylvania, one with a nice pool where we can hang out in the late afternoon. She lies down on a motel towel poolside, and I tell her I'm going back to the room for a moment. I make a quick call to Donovan, who is in New York, ready to meet us in the morning at the school. I allow myself a moment of delight: we're actually pulling off this scheme! But when I return to the pool I find a young man with a scruffy beard and an ominous demeanor talking to Pam. She is obviously flirting with him. I suspect he may be offering her drugs, because she seems annoyed by my return. I pull my towel very close to hers and sit down between them. The man moves to the other side of the pool but continues to watch Pam, who keeps flirting.

I need to get her out of there. I tell her it's time for dinner, and she leaves with me --but not before giving a final glance to this man, who follows us some distance behind. Suddenly, my certainty that we've nearly gotten her to safety is shattered. A new fear that she'll bolt has arisen. I know that if I say anything about this she'll either deny it or run, so I keep my sense of impending danger to myself.

When we return to our room after dinner, the same man is in the hallway outside our room. I lock the door behind us and take the bed nearest the door. Even though I feel inwardly strong, I know I can't possibly physically prevent Pam from leaving if she is determined to do so. The memory of her successful escape from me in Salvador is still fresh.

Pam puts on a nightgown. She keeps going to the window to look out at the man standing outside. I suggest we watch a movie and I pay for *Jumanji*, a story about people playing a game that suddenly comes to life, with man-sized spiders leaping off the game board. I, too, feel trapped in a game I don't understand, with new threats lurking outside the door: I have no idea how to play this game. I offer Pam M&Ms to keep her distracted; even so, she hops up periodically, going to the window to see if he's still there.

And he is. I feel like I'm caught in a horror movie, being tracked by a serial killer who watches our every move, waiting to pounce. I feel this man is my enemy, even though I know the real enemy is something inside my daughter that keeps her fixated on men and drugs, on whatever she imagines they will give her.

I have no idea how to meet this enemy.

I start to pray, only pretending to watch the movie. I pray with everything in me: *"Lord, I don't know what to do. I feel so threatened by the presence of this man. I fear Pam is tempted to go with him. I know there is some terrible force inside my daughter that seeks to destroy her. Please help me know what to do."* I have no idea what action I'll take if she opens the door to go out. All I can do is pray, and so I keep doing that until finally I disappear into the prayer. Calm replaces terror, and I feel spirit entering my body.

Suddenly I know what's required of me. I get up and go out the door, walking briskly toward the man, who leans against the hallway railing facing our door. I stand directly in front of him. My body is shaking, but my voice is firm. "I am this girl's mother," I tell him. "She's a sick girl and needs help. I ask you to leave her alone."

He looks at me with disdain, as if I'm not worth speaking to. He stands erect, a full four inches taller than I am, and stares down at me for another few seconds. I hold my ground. Finally, with a snort, he turns and walks away.

"Is he gone?" Pam asks after I re-enter our room and lean on the door until it clicks.

"Yes, he is."

She yawns and crawls under the covers; in a little while she falls asleep.

I continue to tremble for an hour or more. I do not sleep, yet all night I am living in a horrible nightmare in which an unseen danger threatens to destroy us both. Scenes from *Silence of the Lambs* keep flashing in front of my eyes—scenes of being hunted through dark basement rooms by a serial killer. I am terrified of this nameless predator that stalks my daughter. I know I must remain vigilant even as I also know I am helpless against this enemy.

At the same time, I sense the presence of the power that directed me to do what I could never have done alone: confront a man I perceived as dangerous. All night long I pray to this power: to Christ, to the Mother. At dawn, when I see that the man has not reappeared, I begin to relax.

We leave as soon as I can get Pam awake, and we have breakfast on the road. By the time we're close to the Chapel School, she is asleep again, but she startles awake when we turn onto the bumpy gravel driveway up to the school.

"Where are we?"

"We're going to visit the boarding school I mentioned to you a few weeks ago."

"I'm not interested." She curls up in the seat with her back to me.

She refuses to get out of the car with me when we arrive, so I go in alone to talk with the staff members who are expecting us. They send three girls and a male teacher with me out to the car. They tell Pam to come with them into the school, and say they will help her walk if she needs help. She tries to push them away, but they hold her firmly and lead her to the room where Donovan is waiting for us.

When Pam sees her father there, her jaw drops and her eyes flash. "Dad! What the hell are you doing here—"

I interrupt and say, with forced calmness, "You're going to stay at this school now. They'll help you with some of your problems."

Pam lurches toward me, scowling, and yells, "You lied to me! How could you trick me like that! I hate you." With fists clenched, she moves toward me, and the school personnel quickly usher me and Donovan out the door. As the door closes behind me, I feel triumphant. We've done it!

❧

Pam writes:

When they open the door to that room, I feel my heart drop into my stomach. It's like the feeling you get when the principal calls your name on the loudspeaker, telling you to come to his office, and you know you've done something wrong. Or when you put your glass down on the very edge of the counter and you realize just too late that you missed, and there is no catching it now. You can only watch helplessly as it crashes down. That is what I feel. I still don't really know what's going on, but I know it can't be good.

How do I know this? Not only because of that feeling, but also because, standing behind that door when it opens, is my father. *My father!* He's supposed to be far, far away, in Brazil or somewhere. So I'm very shaken. My brain is so disconnected from reality I can't piece anything together. It's not until they sit me down and explain that this is where I'm going to be staying for a while that I realize how completely I've been tricked. I enter into semishock that will last the whole time I'm there.

After they tell me I'm staying, things start coming together a bit. It becomes clear why there's a suitcase on the table in front of me. I can't believe it! And it gets worse. Much worse. My parents say good-bye, and I yell at them. I tell them I hate them. Little do I know I'm not going to be able to talk to them again for a whole month. They leave, and the posse of Chapel School girls and staff begin to bombard me with details of the new lifestyle I'm going to be leading from now on. The rules go on and on. I have to have "normal" hair, which means letting it grow and no more dying it. No crop tops, no flared jeans, no tank tops, no makeup. This means I literally have nothing to wear.

That is, until I open the suitcase my mother packed for me. It's full of her clothes! Imagine for a second that someone came into your life all of a sudden, and told you that you couldn't be you. That's how I feel. Everything that identifies me has been taken from me, and then I'm told I have to wear my mother's clothes! At this point I'm thinking I'll be able to get out soon. Until they tell me the minimum stay is eighteen months!! That's a year and a half. I can't stand it. I pick up a chair and throw it across the room, screaming, crying, wondering what on earth I can do to get out.

❧

Driving away from the school, I breathe deeply for the first time in several months. I'm delighted to notice that Pam's accusation about my lying produces no guilt, no backlash of familiar self-doubt. I know that I did what had to be done. At the airport where Donovan will start his trip back to Brazil, we eat tuna sandwiches in the minimal lunch room. We share that our bodies feel fifty pounds lighter, that we can even begin to imagine how a relaxed body might feel.

Then I remember that she was gone all weekend "having fun." "Oh, my God, Donovan. What if she's pregnant? What if she has AIDS? If either is true, the school won't keep her."

CHAPTER 9

Tough Love

New York State, June 1996 – December 1998

AFTER a tense week of waiting for test results, the school informs us that Pamela is not pregnant and does not have AIDS! We're so happy she's in a safe place at last, and we're overjoyed to reclaim our own lives.

The school counselor recommends we pay attention to preserving and strengthening our relationship as a couple; an addicted child can ruin a marriage. Too often one parent becomes the enabler (that would be me) and the other feels left out and becomes the critic (that's Donovan). As the parents take opposing roles with the child, they can become estranged. For three long years we have both been so preoccupied with Pam that we've had very little time to enjoy simply being together.

Fortunately, we've built a strong foundation. We met in 1969 at a week-long encounter group at Esalen Institute in California. Sparks flew. We were very attracted to each other—and we fought like crazy. We got married a year and a half later and continued our pattern of alternating closeness and warfare. We made it through that early period and both became more resilient; the relationship grew stronger. We slowly became courageous enough to let our vulnerability show.

Donovan led me to Buddhism, which he had been studying for years. Before we met, he had meditated with a Zen master, and eventually passed a koan test with him. We joined that teacher's *sangha* (spiritual community) and asked him to officiate at our Buddhist wedding ceremony. The vows seemed exactly right to us. We acknowledged that we were walking the spiritual path as a twosome and we committed to being each other's principal support and teacher.

That commitment has endured, even as the outer forms of our path have changed. We developed a serious Zen meditation practice, and then we both trained in bioenergetics, a form of body psychotherapy. Later I led Donovan to the Pathwork, a psychological-spiritual discipline which helped us meet our immature and shadow sides. Together we explored Native American spirituality. More recently, Donovan led me to the *Daime*.

Over time, we settled into complete acceptance of each other exactly as we are.

We've had our portion of hard times. Together we started the Sevenoaks retreat center and weathered several periods of its near collapse, the disintegration of several different incarnations of spiritual community, and the shattering of many illusions about both spirituality and community. And we lived through the death of Donovan's son at the early age of twenty-nine.

But nothing tested our connection as profoundly as having an addicted daughter. We would regularly fight over what was the best way to parent her: he always leaned toward more discipline, which I perceived as lacking heart, and I always veered toward more love, which he saw as permissiveness.

Now, with Pam safely in the Chapel School, we have the respite we need to renew our relationship. We immediately take a beach vacation during which we celebrate our love and rediscover our physical enjoyment of each other. After the earthquake of Pam's addiction roiling our relationship, we are relieved to be back on solid ground, together again.

❧

When we make our first visit to the school, Pam seems overjoyed to see us. "My daughter is back!" I rejoice to myself. Cocaine has loosened its stranglehold on her, and love flows back and forth freely among us. I apologize for having deceived her to get her to the school, and she gives me stunning reassurance: "You did what you had to do... you were right that I was killing myself... I'm sorry for how badly I've treated you."

We make a good connection with Pam's counselor. Donovan asks about the school's success rate: how many students really reform and transform? The counselor answers that it depends on the parents, saying many parents fail to reinforce the school's guidelines so the students backtrack whenever they visit home. These students may not make it. But she affirms that if we really work with the school, they are very confident of success. We promise to work with them one hundred percent.

While many of the school's methods seem strict to me, I accept that this may be exactly what Pam needs. Early on, when she's testing the rules of the school, she refuses to go to a meal and then goes limp when a male teacher directs her to the dining room. He pulls her up the stairs, and she bangs herself up quite a bit while continuing to refuse to go voluntarily. Pam shows me some bruises as she tells me about this incident. I wince, but then listen carefully as she says, "They really mean business here." There's clear admiration in her voice.

They do mean business: Every privilege has to be earned, and every negative act has a consequence. The days are highly structured, beginning with early morning chapel. They allow no flirting between boys and girls, much less dating. The kids eat meals in a designated "family" consisting of a male and female staff member and twelve or so boys and girls grouped together. They are required to eat all the food on their plates, or else it is saved until the next meal. Family meals are a place for discipline; after they've eaten, each student has to "come up for" (talk publicly about) anything they have done wrong. The other family members are invited to add their criticisms. They all go to frequent Alcoholics Anonymous (AA) and Narcotics Anonymous (NA) meetings and work on the Twelve Steps.

Getting to talk with your parents is considered a privilege to be earned. Pam is always grateful to talk with us and appreciates our visits. The school completely turns around her attitude toward us. From the first visit Pam is never again sullen or angry in our presence. We enjoy being with her. We go over with Pam and her counselor a long list of all her major lies and deceits, the stealing and acting-out she has done since she was ten years old. We all agree that lying is her first addiction; all her life it has been very difficult for Pam to own up to her mistakes and admit her deceptions. Coming clean now is still hard for her, but when she witnesses our nonjudgmental acceptance of her confessions, the experience seems to be healing.

Pam tells us she's convinced that without our intervention, she would have ended up a dead addict, a jailed thief, or an institutionalized crazy person. She's telling us exactly what AA also says are the inevitable results of the disease of addiction when left untreated, and it's what we have come to believe. I can't be sure, however, if she's telling us what she really feels or only what she knows she's supposed to say. I've witnessed how adept Pam is at conning adults.

When she earns the right to be with us overnight, we go to a local motel and resume our nightly tradition of singing hymns and praying together. Pam lets her guard down and pleads, "Can't I be somewhere where I can drink *Daime*? The *Daime* helped me connect to God better than anything here at school. I need—"

I interrupt, fearing I'll be swayed by her manipulation. "Pam, this is where you need to be. You're doing so well in school—it's important to finish twelfth grade here. There'll be time later to drink *Daime*. And besides, I thought you liked Father Bill's teaching about God."

"I do like him, but he's not José. I miss José and the *Daime*, terribly."

"Look," I plead, "just finish high school here, while you can. Then anything is possible. Maybe we'll all go back to Brazil to visit after you graduate."

She clams up and doesn't ask again.

🔊

I follow the school's recommendation and go to Al-Anon, the Twelve Step group for families of addicts and alcoholics. I read the literature daily, get a sponsor and attend at least one meeting a week. I also go to open AA and NA meetings to learn more about the disease of addiction from which Pam suffers.

Because both her biological parents had alcohol and drug problems, she always had a severe propensity for addiction. By the time Pam snorted her first hit of cocaine in Salvador, Brazil, at age fourteen, the disease was already seriously life-threatening. Her illness was such that she couldn't experiment with drugs like a normal teenager, nor could she even ease gradually into addiction like some young addicts do. From her first use, she was completely out of control, her life hijacked by addiction to cocaine.

I learn that addiction really is a disease—of body, mind, and soul. The chemistry of an addict/alcoholic is different. Whereas normal people get feedback from their bodies when they've had enough, or get the kinds of hangovers that tell them they've had way too much, the alcoholic/addict never gets this bodily message. In fact, their bodies keep telling them they just need more of that same substance.

The drugs take over their minds, infecting their mental processes with the false belief that the solution to their pain—and then later their guilt about how much pain they are causing themselves and others—is to use more. This makes sense of Pam's telling us in Salvador about getting so drunk she was disoriented, then assuming that what she needed in order to feel better was to drink yet more beer.

Only after the life of the addict demonstrates incontrovertibly just how destructive the use of alcohol and drugs has become can the mind begin to wake up to the reality that ingesting drugs is the problem, not the solution. But as a young teenager Pam couldn't possibly acquire that kind of perspective on her life. She still saw drugs as "fun" and an effective way to numb her psychological pain.

In Al-Anon I also learn more about my own disease of codependence. I hear that I did not cause and cannot cure or control her disease, but I can contribute to it by denial, by holding on to her at any price, or by in any way enabling her use of drugs. I see how I've made my own well-being dependent on her, how I get obsessed with fixing and helping her. I'm told that I need to let her go—to admit that I am powerless over her disease and release her to God.

I also return to therapy, where it becomes clear that wanting connection with Pam at any price relates to the deep, though erroneous, belief I still hold that I was deprived of maternal bonding. I continue my spiritual practice within the *Daime* church ceremonies in Brazil where Donovan and I still go to teach three times a year. Opening further to the presence of the Divine Mother is a major source of healing. When I am with Her, I have all the maternal connection I need.

However, I still judge my own flawed mothering. I believe I should have done a better job with my daughter. My greatest challenge is to not believe my own merciless self-judgments: *You weren't home with her enough. You focused too much on your work. You didn't see Pam clearly as a person with special needs. You didn't enforce consequences for her misbehavior. You didn't protect her enough.*

The belief that brings the most pain is that I should have prevented her sexual abuse at age four. I've played the scene over and over in my mind for years.

My four-year-old daughter was at the pond at Sevenoaks with a babysitter and several other adults who were here for a workshop.

An adult man enticed Pam over to him, pulled out his erect penis, and put her little hand on it. As soon as someone looked in his direction, he swam away.

The event lasted less than five minutes; the impact, a lifetime. Her childhood innocence was destroyed in that moment. She became prematurely and inappropriately fixated on sex. While other children ask for a bedtime story, Pam asked inappropriate questions about sex. Her sleep was disturbed. The crossed eyes she had when she came to live with us—which had self-corrected in the intervening three years—returned. The fragile safety net of trust, carefully woven over her early time of living with us, was ripped apart. I don't know how I can ever forgive myself for letting this happen.

I also berate myself for other traumas in her life: *I should not have let her take the phone call from her birth mother when she was ten. How could I have been so blind about her risky behavior before the rape, or later in Salvador about her cocaine use?*

These repetitive thoughts attack my sense of well-being and eventually undermine my health. I have frequent tension headaches and a chronically knotted, painful lower abdomen. I sense I am holding my woman-parts hostage as self-punishment.

On a warm fall day, Donovan and I take a trip to Virginia Beach, which we pretty much have to ourselves. In our room overlooking the ocean, I fall deep into the pain in my abdomen, which by now has become excruciating. I writhe on the bed and consider an emergency visit to the hospital. Donovan holds my hand, and I confess all the terrible self-judgments that are pounding in my head. The final verdict: BAD MOTHER.

I feel unforgivable. Donovan reminds me, "God's forgiveness is always present. Do you really know better than God?" I am reassured by his calm words, but my belly is still tense and inflamed.

I am compelled to leave the bed by a sudden need to go out into the ocean. I enter the warm waters and feel the soothing presence of Mother Ocean. I pour out my feelings of guilt and unworthiness. I sob. I pound the ocean's surface, flailing my arms. I beg for forgiveness. Finally I lean back into the ocean, letting myself be supported, feeling the immensity of this presence and the smallness of my knotted-up little mind.

As I float on my back, tears streaming, something happens and I finally let go. I receive forgiveness into my being and my body immediately relaxes. I am okay. *I am the mother I am; Pam is the daughter she is.* Nothing could have been otherwise. We are both held in a vast ocean of love. For the next hour I float and swim and cry, floating on this ocean of forgiveness. When I return to the room and to Donovan, I am free of pain. I feel washed clean of my sins.

&

The Chapel School is offering Pam a strong program of behavior modification so she can learn to change her destructive patterns. Their treatment model is based on their beliefs about what is wrong with her. Basically, they view their delinquent students as spoiled brats who need structure and discipline, and to experience consequences for their misbehavior.

I'm happy to cooperate by learning how to be a much stricter mom. We go to classes on "tough love." I throw myself into this approach just as I've hurled myself headlong into all the previous ways I've tried to help Pam.

Early in Pam's life, I worked with a therapist to help Pam bond more fully with me. Since she was abandoned by her mother at an age when even a normal infant experiences separation anxiety, Pam had very little capacity for trust and for sustaining a loving connection. When I had to leave for work I would often came home to a child who acted like I wasn't there. She could be extremely loving one moment and then cut me off the next. Because of my own wounding around the mother-child bond, I would often feel hurt by her rejection of me, instead of recognizing it as the inevitable defense of her vulnerability.

I sought the advice of many experts. One doctor wanted to put her on psychoactive medications; another said they were dangerous and instead recommended nutritional supplements to help change her brain chemistry. The psychiatrist we consulted when she was eleven encouraged us to back off and let only trained professionals talk to her. Other therapists suggested we needed to take on a more active listening role.

Later, José and other shamanic healers we consulted in the *Daime* church were convinced Pam was possessed by negative spirit entities and could only be healed by spiritual means. Some of them recommended letting go of the psychological work and instead engaging in more prayer and ceremony.

The contradictions between various theories about what was going on sometimes overwhelmed me. Everybody had a theory, everybody had a diagnosis, and most were sure they had the only cure.

Each time we found a new therapeutic approach for Pam, we were hopeful of positive change. We wanted to believe that we had finally stumbled upon the solution.

Now, from the experts at the Chapel School we are getting yet another diagnosis and yet another treatment plan. At least the school is truly taking her on, and with full-time help offered in a boarding school setting, it seems like the most promising route we've followed thus far.

ᔥ

Over the two and a half years Pamela stays at the Chapel School, we have frequent meetings with her counselors and teachers. They believe Pam is making steady progress, and we also are convinced. For the first time ever, she's getting good grades, doing wonderful paintings, and beginning to understand math. She has always thought of herself as stupid, but now she's beginning to believe the counselor who frequently reminds her that she's smart. She seems to be enjoying schoolwork and taking pleasure in doing well. We have great hopes that she will finish high school here.

When we visit, we find her honest, respectful of our authority, and genuinely pleased to be in our company. She seems to be getting better. But her outward progress masks her real feelings.

Pam writes:

Everything I do at the Chapel School is a method for getting out. I soon find out that there is no way out, except, apparently, to be real good. But it's kind of tricky. You also have to admit to things that you did wrong in order to be believed.

So I start to make stuff up, big things so I can be applauded for "coming clean." I say I shot someone when we lived in Salvador (I didn't). I say I used cocaine again when I went home for a visit at Christmas (I didn't). I just want to get noticed and, I hope, believed. For one reason only: so I can get out of here.

My two and a half years feel like an eternity. I'm so afraid I'll never get out. It's so painful, I cry every night. A wrenching pain tears through me. The Beach Boys' song "Sloop John B" plays over and over in my head. "I wanna go home, why don't you let me go home?"

But the truth is, when I was home, I didn't want to be there either, so I guess I just don't know what home is... only that this school isn't it.

After two years, Pamela determines that her effort to get out isn't working. She gets terribly depressed and starts cutting herself with razor blades and scissors. She stops trying to cooperate so the school escalates its consequences, including cutting her off from contact with us. Since the school has told us that they almost never give up on anyone, we assume that she'll come around. We are not informed about what's really going on, including the nature of their punishments.

When Pam fights and bites another girl, she is restrained in blankets wrapped with duct tape. When she cuts herself, she is made to sit alone for hours in a room with only the AA "Big Book" for company. When the girls' restroom is trashed and no one "comes up" for it, the entire student body is made to clean the gym floor with their toothbrushes, from dinnertime until one a.m.

Pam loses all respect for the school's authority and becomes utterly defiant. She won't go to class, so she is required to move rocks from one pile to another and back again as punishment. She remains uncooperative.

The school isn't honest with us about what's happening, and Pam isn't allowed to talk with us. We wait, oblivious, hoping for the best.

❧

Then, while Donovan and I are in Brazil teaching, the dreaded call comes. The Chapel School has decided they can no longer keep Pam: they've done all they can and have now given up. We can hardly believe it. These people had promised many times that, as long as we cooperated, they were confident they could turn Pam around. Now they're returning her to us, admitting, "We can't handle her. She's too much for us. She's your responsibility again."

After the call we go to a classy restaurant in the Ipanema section of Rio de Janeiro. I'm so distraught I inadvertently wrap up my false teeth, a partial lower denture, in a napkin that ends up in the restaurant's trash bin. I spend an hour picking through restaurant trash, vainly trying to explain my loss to the curious waiters through my tears and my inadequate Portuguese. Finally I find the denture.

Afterward, we go out to the park of the *Nossa Senhora da Paz*

(Our Lady of Peace) and talk over our options. The counselors at the school recommend either putting her out on the street or getting a court order so she can be mandated to a lockdown facility until she's twenty-one. Both choices seem unbearably harsh.

We take stock: The school hasn't lived up to our hopes for Pam's recovery, but it has kept her off the streets for two and a half of her very vulnerable teenage years, when she might easily have died from a drug overdose. For all this time she has had no drugs or sex, and we know that she could never have abstained without the intense structure of this school. Being there, Donovan and I agree, probably saved her life. And she learned that she's smart and can do well in school if she applies herself. She also learned a lot, at least intellectually, about the disease of addiction and the Twelve Steps of AA.

But her deeper psychological problems remain completely untouched. She didn't trust the people at the school; she felt they treated the students with judgment and criticism, and that their punishments were humiliating. Without a foundation of trust, she could never really open up enough emotionally to do the psychological work to effect real change. She felt limited to two options: submit to their authority or rebel. There was no opportunity to develop her own integrity, so she retreated into her defenses of defiance, withdrawal, and dishonesty.

Nor did she grow spiritually. The school's conventional religious instruction didn't penetrate to the spiritual level she had already experienced in her *Daime* work. Her connection with God has not deepened, but her distrust has. Her hatred of authoritarian adults has solidified. And now, Pamela, at seventeen and a half years old, is back in our laps again. We are at a loss.

CHAPTER 10

Sent By the Moon

Omaha, Nebraska, January – April 1999

WHERE can Pam go? Back to our house? We live in the middle of a retreat center. People come here to do personal inner healing, expecting an atmosphere of safety and calm. Pam's behavior is so unpredictable, and so potentially destructive, that Donovan is certain we can't risk having her here. Reluctantly, I have to agree.

During the time Pam has been away at school, the Brazilian *Daime* church has established a strong community within driving distance of us. A Brazilian woman named Helena runs this church, which has a mostly American following. Helena has told us several times that she thinks we should bring Pam back into the *Daime*. Pam's godparents, John and Anne, have become leaders in this church community, devoted both to the church and to Helena, and they are willing to take Pam into their house to live.

But Helena runs her church like a spiritual boot camp. Having watched Pam thoroughly rebel against the tight structure of the Chapel School, and even against the looser structure of the Brazilian *Daime* community in Mauá, Donovan thinks it is unlikely that she would adjust to the discipline of Helena's church.

When we call Pam at school, she doesn't ask to come home or to live in the *Daime* community. Instead, she sobs into the phone, "I want to go live with my real dad."

Her biological father, Tom, is now in recovery and goes regularly to AA meetings. He has maintained contact with Pam over the years, and even visited her once at our house. Still, we're surprised when he tells us he's ready to try having her live with him and his new wife in Omaha, Nebraska. We go over some of Pam's recent history with him, warning him that while she's been completely sober at the boarding school, we don't know if she can maintain it outside of that structure. But we also know that Tom knows what alcoholics and addicts are like and might be better attuned to her issues than we are, having been there himself. We are relieved and grateful, and decide it's probably our best option.

℘

I pick Pam up from the Chapel School on a bitterly cold New Year's Day, 1999. Two days later Donovan, Pam, and I fly to Omaha. By the time school starts there, after vacation, we have her well established in her own room in Tom and his wife's mobile home, and she's registered at a small private high school nearby.

We plan to visit Pam over Easter, the first weekend in April; we hope that reconnecting with us then might give her the boost she'll need to complete the school year. But by March she begins to complain: "It's not working out here. I'm bored with school, I don't want to finish. I want to go live with friends." Tom and his wife are frustrated by a new wave of uncooperative behavior. Donovan immediately flies out to visit her, and afterward Pam seems more grounded. She says she's willing to give it another try.

Oddly, none of us comes to the obvious conclusion that she might have started using drugs again.

I still want to go visit Pam over the Easter weekend, but Donovan feels strongly that we need to give her more time on her own there to work it out with Tom and his wife. We decide, instead, to do an Easter retreat for ourselves.

We plan to attend the *Daime* work held on the Thursday before Easter, the night of Christ's trial at Gethsemane—the pivotal moment of surrender to His fate that sets the Easter story in motion. The first time I visited Brazil I had done this work, and had been overwhelmed with the terror of surrendering my personal will. Letting go felt like death, and I could not move beyond my fear. Now I'm hoping that I'll be ready to experience greater surrender.

During the ceremony, I keep hearing Pam's voice, loud and insistent, pleading with me: "Please, let me come back and join the *Daime* church." I recall her substantial connection to the *Daime* in Brazil. I am once again swept with faith that the *Daime* sacrament is the power of divine love distilled into liquid form. I know that this power can transform anything. I sense the presence of Christ as the healer who could exorcise demons from those who had faith in him, and I pray that Pam might be ready to be cleansed of her demons.

At the same time, I have doubts. I don't fully trust the voice I'm hearing or the faith I'm feeling. I try to calm myself, spending time at the altar absorbing the energy of the icon of the Divine Mother on the table, and enjoying the daffodils arrayed there. I am nourished by God's love emanating from these small golden trumpets.

When I tell Donovan what I've heard during the work, he's skeptical. Even though we're friends with John and Anne, we're not close with Helena. Donovan is convinced that Pam is not ready, that she would rebel against the ceremonial rules and fail to benefit from the healing work done in this particular church.

On Good Friday evening, I call Omaha. Tom tells me Pam has left with her boyfriend. He says he was annoyed and suspicious as they left, and he pressed Pam about when she would return. When she replied, "Midnight," her curfew time, he let her go. I have a sinking feeling in my gut but dismiss it as my ever-present anxiety. I am haunted by the fact that it's Good Friday, traditionally a dark day spiritually.

The next morning Tom calls to tell me she hasn't come home. At 5:30 a.m., he says, he filed a runaway report with the police, who told him that since she's nearly eighteen, there was little they could do. Later that day he calls again, this time reporting that Pam has called him, explaining her whereabouts by saying she spent the night with her boyfriend and passed out. She maintains this has nothing to do with drugs or alcohol. Tom responds, "Bullshit," and tells her to come home. But she defies him, saying she and her boyfriend are going to a car show.

Tom fully expects her to return by the end of the weekend, so there's nothing to do but wait. I play a piece of music that repeats, as a chant, the words of Jesus at Gethsemane: *Stay here and keep watch with me. Watch and pray.*[1] As I pray, some peace comes to me, and with it a resolve to bring Pam to the *Daime* church again.

However, when I share this with Donovan, he points out that I am once again fantasizing that I can be the instrument of Pamela's healing. He reminds me that she must save herself; I can't do it. We have already talked to the counselors at the Chapel School, and they have made clear that they believe we should do nothing until Pam asks for help. My Al-Anon friends have advised the same. Nonetheless, I find my heart is brimming as it holds close the healing potential of the *Daime*.

Pam does not return to Tom's home on Sunday. On Monday he and his wife decide that they simply can't handle her, and should she return they will declare her "out of control" so she can be placed in a foster home. We get from Tom the number of a friend of Pamela's in Omaha with whom she stayed on Saturday night. The friend tells us she no longer has any idea where Pam is.

---

[1]Taizé music from the CD *Laudate*.

I call the law firm in Omaha that had helped us adopt Pam there seventeen years ago, hoping their lawyer for juveniles will give me some options. But he repeats that since she's so close to eighteen, we really have no legal options. He recommends a private investigator who can help us find her if we want to do so. That night my Al-Anon group urges me to let go and do nothing, to wait until she's ready to ask for help.

🌙

Around midnight Tuesday, after we're both asleep, Pam calls collect.

"Where are you, Pam? Are you safe? Are you OK?" I'm struggling to remember what I know about crisis intervention—trying to keep her on the line, not wishing to say anything that would make her hang up abruptly.

"I'm okay. I've got my own apartment. Someone loaned it to me. It was really dirty but I cleaned it up." She pauses. Then, sounding teary, she adds, "Last night a tornado hit here... but I was so fucked up I slept through the whole thing."

"I'm so glad you're okay. But, Pam, you need help..." I plead, my voice trailing off, not knowing what to say next.

"I know," she sniffles.

I ask, "Can you get out of the situation where you are? Is it dangerous?"

"No, it's not. I'll go back to Tom's house tomorrow."

"Good, Pam, I'm glad to hear that."

And then, abruptly, she concludes, "I have to stop talking now. 'Bye."

I feel better after the call; at least she's alive.

ᔥ

But Pam doesn't return to Tom's. The next evening I talk with Tom's wife, who skewers me with judgment and blame, saying that Pamela is obviously a very sick girl and we were wrong to send her to live with them.

I feel worse and worse, roiled in deep waves of shame. How could I have been so selfish—or so naive? How could I have been so out of touch with what was really going on with Pam? I feel on the edge of madness, floating in a burning sea of self-condemnation, fear, and utter helplessness: "bad mother" hell. I sit at our home altar for hours, but nothing changes, so I get up and go to bed. I lie on my back, repeating the Serenity Prayer. Finally I fall into a fitful sleep.

After perhaps an hour's sleep, I awake feeling startled and disoriented. I'm drawn to the window where I'm immediately transfixed by a very bright half-moon. Now I feel strangely, almost supernaturally calm, and I have the unmistakable sensation that the moon's brightness is pouring into me through my crown chakra. As the light pours in, understanding comes with it. My Divine Mother, in the form of the moon, is talking to me. She is speaking, but not with words, and I am listening, but not with ears. My whole body is drinking in what is being communicated.

She's bringing me to a deeper level of surrender to love than I have ever experienced before. At that moment, I know that serving love is all I ever want to do, and that if I follow love with all my heart, nothing else matters. I also know that I will go to Omaha, and with the help of the Mother, seek Pamela. And if it is God's will, I will find her and bring her back to live in the *Daime* community.

The outer me is dubious about finding Pam, and uncertain that she would come with me even if I did. I also continue to have doubts about this *Daime* group and its leader, Helena. Further, I'm concerned about losing my place in the Pathwork spiritual group, of which I am a leader, because many of the Pathwork teachers disapprove of the *Daime* church. But most central to my concerns is my fear of alienating Donovan, who so dislikes the idea of my going to Omaha and attempting to bring Pam back.

At this moment, though, all these concerns and doubts do not matter. All that matters is that I serve the truth that is being called forth by my Mother, the moon. All that matters is that I merge with the master of love, Christ, who will lead me where I need to go. Only by risking all to follow Truth will I ever be truly free. I know all this without a shred of doubt. My resolve is clear, and my whole being is immensely calm from the inside out. I will do as instructed, whatever the cost. I return to bed and sleep soundly.

In the morning I talk to the private investigator in Omaha. He has a reputation for being very aggressive, and it's no lie. First, he refuses to work with me unless I have a lawyer. I tell him that's fine. Then he barks, "It's a one-in-a-million chance. But we can talk." I will not be put off by his attitude. I tell him I'll meet him in Omaha that evening as soon as I arrive. As non-reassuring as he is, he impresses me: If anyone can get this job done, he can.

🦋

On the way out the door to catch the plane to Omaha, I pick up a letter I've just received from my godson Christopher in prison. Chris is a forty-two-year-old African-American man whom I had semi-adopted when he was a young child. For years I thought he might be the closest I would come to having a child of my own. In more ways than one, he's a soul-brother to Pam.

When he was seven years old, Chris took some costume jewelry from a friend of mine. I confronted him and he declared, "I'm going to keep stealing until I have everything I want." I assured him that, unlike his fantasy, this would only guarantee a life in jail. I accompanied him to the police station after his first arrest for shoplifting when he was nine years old. He spent the rest of his childhood in reform school.

As a young adult, Chris fell victim to the inner-city crack cocaine epidemic and continued stealing and using drugs for many years, spending much of his adulthood in prison. But we always stayed in touch. I supported his sporadic efforts to get clean, and he always considered me his god-mother.

Now he's been through a long-term drug treatment program in prison and is also getting vocational training there. He seems serious—perhaps for the first time—about turning his life around.

Chris writes:

Dear Susan,

I know deep in my heart that God put you in my life to help me learn that I am worthwhile and lovable, something I didn't believe for all my years of growing up in the projects with no one to guide me.

Before I met you I thought I was just a throwaway kid only meant for a life of hustling, stealing and carrying on just to survive. I felt my life would end up the same as so many others that I've known—dead or in prison. I never thought I would ever know the meaning of a happy family.

I have found my own way through the storm by knowing that I had your prayers to push me when I felt like giving up. I know that someday I will be able to give something back to you.

Love always,

Your God Son Christopher

Chris's letter is coming just when I need it. He reminds me that I can hold out hope to Pamela even though she may have lost faith in herself.

❧

For the remainder of the two flights to Omaha, I immerse myself in the only book I've brought with me: *Love Without Conditions: Reflections on the Christ Mind* by Paul Ferrini. I read, then pray and meditate. I find I'm in a deeply altered state, feeling divine love flowing through me and assenting to being an instrument of God's peace. I read the words Ferrini says are channeled from the Christ: "Stop pretending that the door is locked. I am here at the threshold. Reach out and take my hand and we will open the door and walk through together.... I am the door to love without conditions. When you walk through, you too will be the door."

What does it matter that the "door" to Pam's salvation appears locked? If Love is leading, nothing can remain closed. I continue reading: "One person is no more worthy or unworthy of love than another.... This is the kind of love I offer you and that I ask you to extend to others." I think of Chris and how I have loved him.

I also love Pam unconditionally, and I cannot stop loving her just because she behaves abysmally and even cruelly toward me, herself, and others. It is not a love that can be thwarted by outer conditions. It is not a love that I prove by doing anything. It is simply what I am. With eyes closed, breathing deep into the space of the heart, I keep dropping further inside, feeling the pool of love in my heart widen and deepen, expanding until it becomes a vast impersonal ocean. Then even the ocean drops away and there is nothing, nothing except this presence, this love that has no form and no beginning and no end. Only this.

As we land in Omaha, I find myself repeating a mantra that comes to me spontaneously: "There is only love and forgiveness. All else is illusion."

CHAPTER 11

Cops and Robbers

Omaha, Nebraska, April 1999

I GO straight from the airport to Taylor's office. He looks and sounds the movie role part of a private investigator. Handsome, wiry, with light hair and intense blue eyes, sucking a cigar, he speaks with a mixture of experience, bravado, and self-aggrandizement. He introduces me to his assistant, an attractive, tough-talking young blond woman with a personal history of drug abuse and work in juvenile facilities. Wendy is very savvy about the drug scene in Omaha and will work closely with me.

Taylor is convinced that Pam has already been taken in by a gang. He says there are over a hundred gangs in Omaha, mostly run from Los Angeles, which regularly recruit runaways. It's likely she is being used for prostitution. The pimps, he tells me, will control her behavior. And he braces me for a harsh reality: I need to know that we are dealing with dangerous, armed characters, not just a seventeen-year-old runaway. Unless she really wants to get away from this frightening scene, there isn't much chance of rescuing her.

He has two immediate recommendations. First, we need to obtain a court order, which will authorize him to be an officer of the law so he can do whatever is necessary to apprehend Pam. Second, I need a cell phone so he and I can be in immediate contact at any time, night or day. He gives me phone numbers for himself and Wendy.

Wendy helps me locate a place to rent a cell phone that, mercifully, stays open for me past its usual closing time. Then we drive past the lower-middle-class suburban area where a teacher from her school had seen Pam two days earlier. Wendy promises to go back to this neighborhood tonight with pictures of Pam, to canvass the local residents and see if she can get any leads.

I go back to Tom's house in the mobile home park, exhausted. The next morning I call Taylor to see what I can do to be useful. Wendy's time in the neighborhood has yielded no information, so he says there's nothing we can do except wait for the legal papers, which he needs before he can act. I call the lawyer's office to discover that all the lawyers are out until afternoon—and no one has heard of the papers Taylor said he sent over. Feeling frustrated and powerless, I cannot think clearly, nor can I seem to access my intuition.

I pray again to release Pam to love and to let go of any self-importance attached to my role in the drama of her life. Then I walk around the lake at the center of the park. The crisp early spring air, the crocuses and daffodils, and the presence of water help calm my mind so I can think more clearly.

While walking, I snap into recognition that if these papers Taylor wants are to become reality, I'm the one who needs to make that happen. It's already Friday morning, and unless we get these papers today, we'll have to wait until after the weekend. I resolve to get another copy of them from Taylor and to sit in the lawyer's office until we have them completed. I also realize that I need to go to Pam's school, talk to the principal, and ask her to alert the students and faculty to call me or Taylor immediately if anyone sees Pam. I confirm my plan with Taylor and drive to the school.

The principal, Mrs. Brown, is gracious and tells me that Pam has never given them any trouble concerning rules or boundaries; I remember how convincingly Pam conned those in authority at the Chapel School. Mrs. Brown shares more details about the teacher's sighting of Pam. As I'm about to leave, the principal says that she thinks Pam called her friend Abby a time or two. It occurs to me, as a long shot, to ask Mrs. Brown to tell Abby to let Pam know —should she call again—that I'm in town and to give her my cell phone number.

On the way to Taylor's I pass a Catholic church of St. Mary Magdalen and feel drawn to stop. In an alley next to the church, I give over to prayer, beseeching Christ, the Divine Mother and Mary Magdalen to help me locate my daughter. I sing a few *Daime* hymns. I hear an inner voice—which I believe is the voice of the *Daime*—calmly reassuring, "Just bring her to me. I will do the rest."

But the distance between where I am now—a back alley in Omaha, Nebraska—and any *Daime* church community seems insurmountable. I cry softly, but as I do I feel my chest softening with the sweet feeling of love and the certainty that what feels formidable to me is nothing for Christ. If it is God's will, she will be found.

At Taylor's office I pick up copies of the court papers, then drive over to the lawyers' offices. All of them are at lunch. Sitting in a sub shop across the street from the offices, I hit my lowest point. I know that if we don't locate her—and she is lost to the streets indefinitely— the hardest thing I will have to live with is the fact that I didn't go to Omaha on Easter weekend when my heart called me to do so. I will have to forgive myself all over again and it won't be easy.

Sitting on a hard wrought-iron garden chair, staring out a plate glass window at a busy downtown Omaha street, I narrow my focus to the present moment, carefully chewing and experiencing each bite of my sandwich. I let the tears fall and keep my awareness in the moment—on the inhale and exhale of breath, on the sensation of wet tears on my cheeks, and on chewing and tasting each bite. Focusing my awareness here and now is all that keeps me sane.

⅏

I enter the lawyers' offices at 1:45 p.m. and tell the secretary that I will stay until someone can see me. About ten minutes later I hear her say to an attorney who has just returned from lunch, "There's a woman here in urgent need of a lawyer." True enough! Finally, the firm's attorney for juveniles sees me in the conference room. Mr. Terry Blundon is formal, and perhaps has decided to humor me. But he informs me that there would be no jurisdiction for such a case in Nebraska.

I'm momentarily bewildered. Then something clicks, and I pull out copies of Pam's adoption papers, reminding him that she had been formally adopted in this state. He agrees to call a probate judge but cautions me not to be optimistic, because it's unlikely the judge will be willing to assume jurisdiction. I sit in the waiting room until Blundon calls me back only to tell me, "This judge cannot hear such a case." He has no further suggestions.

I drive back to Taylor's office to talk the situation over with him. He suggests going another route: approaching the juvenile judge and filing a "child in need" petition. Since Pam is so close to eighteen years old, they might not accept the petition, but it's worth a shot; we have no other options. So I return to the law firm and pressure Mr. Blundon to consider this. He insists that it's not likely to work, but tells me that if I demand it, he'll give it a try. I face him squarely and say, "Yes, please try." With a sigh, he goes to work on yet another set of papers. I go back to confer with Taylor.

Blundon calls on my cell phone when the papers are nearly ready, and I race back to his office, determined to go with him to the juvenile court for the judge's signature. We leave his office at 4:05 p.m., after the courts are already officially closed. As we're driving, his formal manner softens and we start to use first names. Terry asks questions about Pam, and I share some of the significant stories, glad to have a sympathetic ear. We arrive at the courthouse at 4:25 p.m. Even though I know that court is no longer in session, I feel unexpectedly serene.

As I get out of the car, I'm suddenly aware that we're not alone.

There is a spirit being standing just in front of us: an angel? Christ? As we head toward the courthouse, I find that I'm walking about two paces behind this being of light. He is leading the way; I need only follow. I feel completely calm and confident. As long as He's preceding me, I feel sure the right thing will happen. When we enter the courthouse on the ground floor, the policeman tells us he thinks all the judges have gone home, but he invites us to go upstairs if we want to.

We find one judge working late—a pleasant-looking, middle-aged African-American woman. I warm to her right away. We tell our story, and without hesitation she signs the orders. The entire process takes less than five minutes. Pam is now officially a ward of the state of Nebraska and ordered into immediate treatment at Charter Psychiatric Hospital whenever she is found. The papers empower Taylor as an officer of the court so he can do whatever he needs to do to pick her up. As we leave the courthouse, Terry admits to being astonished that we so easily achieved our goal. I know that "we" haven't done it, but I don't risk saying who did.

By 4:50 p.m. Taylor has the papers he needs, and allows himself a moment of delight, then resumes his tough-guy mask. "Okay, good. Now we need to find this girl."

At 5:15 p.m., just as I'm pulling out onto a major thruway during the height of Friday rush hour, my cell phone rings. Fumbling with one hand through the many things in my backpack, I finally wrestle it out. It's Pam.

"How are you?" I blandly ask.

"I'm fine," she replies. "What are you doing here?"

"I'm here to see you, Pam. I'd really like to see how you are, take you out for a meal, talk about what you need. Where are you? Can we get together?"

"I'm busy tonight. Maybe tomorrow."

Then she asks, "How's Mark? I think about him a lot." Mark is the other young American who was with her in the Brazilian *Daime* community. He's now in recovery and part of the U.S. *Daime* church community.

"Mark's fine," I reply. "Would you like to see him? Maybe we could fly together back to the *Daime* community. Would you like that?"

"Maybe," she answers blankly.

I try again. "How about getting together tonight to talk? I can meet you anywhere you say."

"Okay, I guess I could."

"Great, where?"

"There's an AA meeting at the Sunnyside shopping center. Do you know where that is?"

"I'll find it. When can I meet you there, Pam?"

"How about if I meet you at eight?

"Okay, great. I'll see you then."

We've been on the phone about five minutes. As I press the "off" button, I see that my hand is trembling. I dial Taylor. He wants me to come to his office immediately to plan our strategy, but I've got Tom's car, and first I have to pick him up and take him home.

Another scheme is bubbling up in my mind, as I wonder if I really need Taylor's help after all. Pamela had sounded so much better than I expected; maybe she'd meet me as she said she would and let me take her back with me. When I pick up Tom and tell him that I'm planning to meet Pam that night, he says he doubts she'll follow through.

Back at Tom's place, I'm still torn. Do we really need this cops-and-robbers scenario Taylor is anticipating? I try to reach Donovan by phone, finally locating someone who pulls him out of a meeting. He is simple, clear, direct: "Don't try to manage this on your own." Point taken.

Then I replay in my mind something Blundon said: she can't legally leave Omaha at this point no matter how willing she might be, because she's a ward of the state and she's been mandated to Charter hospital. I once again thank whatever divine beings are in charge of this child's destiny, for making a murky path clear.

✍

I arrive at Taylor's about 7:00 p.m., and he starts laying out several strategies. He intends to have police back-up available. If Pam arrives in a car with several guys, he will assume they're armed and dangerous, and call the police to surround the car. If Pam refuses to get out, we'll need the police to corner the car so it can't leave. If, on the other hand, she's willing to go with me, I'll take her up to the upper level of the shopping center, telling her I've parked Tom's car up there with my purse in it. That way, we can put some distance between us and the car she arrives in, and we're less likely to be followed and harassed.

He and Wendy remind me of her probable drugged state. She's only thinking about drugs and a good time now; she's not in her right mind. He suggests she might call and cancel our rendezvous, in which case I am to plead with her, tell her how badly I need to see that she's all right. I should say I want to make sure she has some good food in her. Above all, I should offer her money: any addict will respond to that.

The longer they talk, the more I realize that I've slipped back into denial about the reality of her drug use. I've again forgotten that the person talking to me on the phone is not my child who loves me, but a drug addict who only knows how to manipulate for advantage. I accept their wisdom about the need to plan for all possibilities. And I accept the assumption that, in her present state, Pam is not available to reason, or to love.

Taylor, Wendy, and I leave his office in his red van with blackened windows. In the driver's seat, Taylor is talking on his cell to his associate investigator, who is already at the mall checking things out. Taylor is the indisputable commanding officer in charge of this small company, and his word is law. As we discuss battle plans, I realize that my role is simply to execute his orders. I vow to do as I'm told so this drama can be carried out flawlessly.

We arrive at the parking lot of the upper mall, and Taylor directs me to get into the blue pickup, also with darkened windows, that his associate is driving.

I plug my cell phone, which is almost out of juice, into his cigarette lighter and almost immediately my phone rings. It is exactly 7:30 p.m., and Pam is on the phone, wanting to cancel our meeting. Remembering Taylor's instructions, I urge her to meet me, first promising food, and then money. She pauses and responds, "You want to give me money?" I repeat that I do. Sure enough, this changes everything. I hear her speaking with someone else in the room. She comes back on the line and tells me she has a ride and will arrive at the mall soon. I hang up and sigh deeply, releasing the accumulated tension in my chest.

Wow, I think. *Thank God for Taylor telling me to offer money!*

We relay to Taylor what Pam has said by cell phone. Then his associate and I drive around to the lower mall a short distance from where the AA meeting is being held. About ten minutes later we see a small black car--again with darkened windows--drive slowly by the meeting's entrance. We all spot it. It circles around and parks a little distance away. Taylor, who has Pam's picture with him, drives by the car and confirms that she's in it. Then he directs the blue truck to the upper level of the mall, where I am let out, leaving my purse behind.

I start walking, praying hard and paying attention to every step so I don't wobble, slowly moving toward the lower level of the mall. The black car circles closer, and when I'm directly in front of the AA entrance, it stops.

Pam gets out of the passenger side and walks toward me. She's wearing a see-through white lace scoop-neck blouse with a black bra underneath and heavy makeup. Her hair is cut very short and she's smoking a cigarette, with a pack and lighter in her hand. She looks cheap, but my heart leaps upon seeing her. We hug briefly. I notice three small gashes on her upper left arm and wonder what they mean.

"Where's the money?" she asks immediately.

"My purse is in Tom's car on the upper level here. Let's walk up there and talk a little. It's good to see you, Pam."

She seems reluctant, wary. We walk about ten feet in the direction of the upper level of the shopping center.

"How are you doing?"

"I'm fine. I could use some money though. Everything's okay." Pam glances nervously back at the black car.

"I have money for you, Pam. Come with me and we'll get it."

Just then, Wendy gets out of the red van and approaches us, placing herself firmly between Pam and the black car.

"Hi," she says softly, doing a good job of appearing uncertain. "Do you folks happen to know where the AA meeting is?"

"Oh yeah," Pam volunteers cheerily, "it's right over there."

"Thanks," Wendy replies, glancing over at the entrance and then fixing her gaze back on Pam. "So, are you going? Have you been there before? This is, like, my first time."

Pam blinks and looks at me, momentarily distracted from getting her money, before replying to Wendy, "Oh, I used to. I don't need it anymore."

Wendy smiles, as if she's playing for time. I tense up, starting to wonder what's going on when the side door of the van slides open and Taylor hops out, grabs Pam's arm, and shows her his badge.

"I'm an officer of the court and you're coming with us."

"Oh, *fuck*!" Pam shrieks, glaring at me furiously.

With Wendy's firm grip on her other arm, the two of them guide Pam through the open door of the van and into the rear, padded with a mattress. Taylor directs me to sit in one of the two swivel seats in the back. Wendy takes the one nearest the van door, slamming the door shut. Taylor heads toward the driver's side of the black car.

Pam's face is twisted in rage. "I can't believe you'd do this to me," she shrieks. "Again! Just like the Chapel School. What are you going to do to me now—lock me up until I'm twenty-one? I can't believe I fell for it again!"

"I'm afraid this is my last chance, Pam," I mumble. "I had to do it."

Pam breaks down into sobs, her shoulders heaving. "I need to... I need to talk to Mark... I have to talk to him," she stammers between sobs.

I repeat what I'd told her earlier on the phone. "Maybe that will be possible." Abiding by Taylor's rules, I fall silent.

Wendy takes up the slack. "I know you're pissed now, Pam, but later on you'll thank your mom." She tells Pam about having been an addict herself, and creates an opening. With shaking hands, Pam lights a cigarette.

Pam starts spewing a laundry list of what she's been taking— drinking a lot of beer and margaritas daily, smoking marijuana as well as a pack and a half of cigarettes daily. She's also been doing crack cocaine, which, even in her present state, she says she knows is highly addictive. "It doesn't even make you feel all that good," she says. "But you get the hit right away, and it just makes you want to do more."

Taylor returns to the van and starts the engine. We're on our way. Pam lights another cigarette. She keeps asking where we're going and how long she'll be locked up. At some point I say, "Pam, you're going to be eighteen soon, and after that, there's nothing I can do."

We're most of the way to the hospital when Taylor volunteers, "We're going to Charter mental hospital where you can detox and get your head back on straight." She calms down a bit after that, though she continues to chain-smoke. Oddly, she's concerned about not spilling ashes on the mattress. Wendy gives her a cup to use as an ashtray.

By the time we arrive at the hospital, Taylor has quietly phoned Donovan in Virginia and Tom in Omaha to let them both know what has happened. He's also alerted the hospital that we're on our way, and that we have a court order mandating her admission. On either side of

Pam, Taylor and Wendy escort her through a steel door with a small window, and I follow. The door locks behind us.

৯

Wendy and I sit with Pam for a long time in the admitting room. We talk about Wendy's past and Pam's runaway stories. Finally a doctor arrives and starts asking questions—really *stupid* questions, it seems to me. "Do you have trouble sleeping?" (She wasn't sleeping at all at night, just partying, maybe sleeping a few hours during the day.) "Do you feel anxious?" (She wasn't feeling much of anything, high as she was all the time.) "Do you have trouble relating to people?" (Not at all. She just has sex with anybody male. Why bother with relationships?) Then, seemingly endless questions about her medical history, allergies, inoculations, and so on.

About two hours later, we finally go back to the adolescent unit where a nurse asks most of the same questions all over again and takes some blood for drug and alcohol testing. Pam has been very forthright about all her drug and alcohol use; I doubt the tests will show anything she hasn't already told us.

I leave Pam in a private room with a bath, noting what a ritzy place this is compared to the Chapel School with its trailers and four or five girls to a room. I vaguely wonder what it costs here. I drive home exhausted yet exhilarated. What an incredible day's work! While driving home to Tom's, I pray out loud, offering praise and gratitude, and singing hymns of joy.

CHAPTER 12

Sexual Possession

Omaha and Washington, D.C., April – June 1999

I VISIT Pam in the hospital the next day. Her face is pasty-white with green patches; detox is in full swing with nausea, dizziness, and exhaustion. She can't bear to talk to anyone, so I leave her some clothes and go home.

The next morning I'm uncertain whether to visit, so I talk to a staff member on the phone. She is very sweet and supportive, literally saying, "I feel your pain," and about Pam, "poor girl." Hers is an entirely different response from that of the Chapel School staff, with their intense morality, their punishments, and their single-minded advice to parents about tough love. Here, it's all sweetness and sympathy, which strikes me as both incredibly naive yet also a welcome balm for my terribly bruised self-esteem. She urges me to come see Pam and says she or another social worker will be around to help us talk together if we need it.

Pam is up for conversation; we don't need any help. We go to her room and sit on her bed. She lays the story out straight. Last Friday she'd been with her boyfriend of six weeks and they'd drunk beer, snorted cocaine, and had sex for the first time. He left the next morning and she hasn't seen him since. She spent Saturday night with her friend Abby, then left on Sunday afternoon and went to a gas station, intent on picking up someone. She succeeded: a man named Scott who had recently been released from prison for attempted murder.

He set Pam up in an apartment he used for parties, which was filthy so she cleaned it. Scott started procuring men for Pam, and she started "working." One day she made $800. She spent it all on crack cocaine.

At this point in Pam's story, I'm barely breathing.

"Pam, wait, I can't hear any more now," I say, falling back on the bed. Tears sting my eyes, and I repeat out loud several times, "Holy Mary, Mother of God."

When I can sit up again, I ask Pam to continue her story. She says she's not been using protection most of the time. She hopes she isn't pregnant, but will keep the baby if she is. Crack is a terrible drug, she says, and she really wants to be free of it.

I finally pop the question that has been on my mind for days now. "Pam, would you like to come back east with me, live with John and Anne and the kids, and drink *Daime* again?"

"Maybe," she hedges. "Yes, maybe so."

She really wants to talk to Mark, her friend from the Mauá community who is now in recovery in the States. Like him, she isn't attracted to a "normal" life. She's drawn to the drug culture because of its simplicity: "There's only one thing to think about," she admits, "where to get your next drugs." She is drawn to the intensity, the immediacy of the drug "fellowship," where she is instantly connected and no one judges you. She likes being part of an outlaw fellowship. She uses her hands as she talks, physically placing the drug subculture below normal relationships. The only other thing that attracts her, she says, is the *Daime* family, and she moves her hands above the level of the normal world. Both cultures are intense, interconnected communities where people take care of one another. I briefly interject that drug "friends" aren't real friends, because everyone is only out for themselves. She nods her head in agreement, but insists that normal relationships don't interest her.

Then she talks more about her extreme, split nature—the crack and other drugs on the downside and the attraction to purity, goodness, and love of God on the upside. The spirits of the *Daime* pull her upward toward the light, whereas the spirits of the crack drag her down into darkness. She tells me she hates being controlled by the drugs, but doesn't know how to stop. We both agree that the *Daime* is the only medicine that might be strong enough to counter the allure of cocaine.

She says she knows she needs to be away from teenagers, even normal teenagers, as most of them casually use alcohol or pot and have sex. She tells me she can't use anything or have any sex if she's going to heal. "I need to be around good people," she says, "a pure lifestyle, wearing white and singing hymns." Her bipolar extremes are plain to see. Still, I can't repress a thrill in my heart at her willingness to return to drinking *Daime*. I only hope we can make it come true.

🙊

Donovan arrives in Omaha the next day and Pam is altogether different as she talks to him: hard, cut-off, cool. Now she says she doesn't think she's ready to change. She isn't ready to give up what she fears she'd have to—boys, sex, drugs, makeup, sexy clothes, and short hair—if she came back to the *Daime*. She isn't ready, hasn't hit bottom yet, isn't ready to turn it around. We'd rescued her once again, but it hadn't been her decision to seek help. She says she's pretty sure that even if we take her back now, she'd leave us when she turns eighteen. So why don't we just let her go back to the streets here until she's ready to ask for help? She doesn't feel finished with her scene in Omaha, or with her friends, and she'd like us to take her back where we picked her up.

Pam is echoing the basic message I'd heard in Al-Anon, and it's hard to dispute. If she isn't ready, no amount of help or even drinking *Daime* can change her. My heart sinks. Donovan feels she is speaking the truth. He had been especially affected by her confession to him that when she first saw cocaine, even before he went out to visit her, she immediately used the drug. She seems to have no capacity to resist temptation.

On the other hand, I feel Pam is in a state of deep defense against the possibility of healing and change, and that's why she's telling Donovan she isn't ready. Hope is such a fragile thing and makes one feel so vulnerable. I see that she's scared of that vulnerability, scared of once again trying something and failing. She has so much trouble believing in herself, especially in front of Donovan, whom she fears she will always disappoint yet again. From my point of view she's hedging, hiding her hope, and staying "safe" in the familiar feeling of being a failure.

We leave the hospital divided. Donovan feels we've done all we can, and unless we can find a lock-up place for her until she is twenty-one, probably nothing we do will have much effect.

I still feel sure she is supposed to come to the *Daime*. But I also feel lonely and deeply insecure. I pray a lot, and keep coming back to the *Daime*. How could we not offer her this incredible opportunity, one that is available to so few other parents? Even if she just did a few ceremonies, the *Daime* would counter the effects of the crack cocaine now clouding her brain. At the very least, the inner battle for her soul would be engaged.

That afternoon I call Mark, tell him the barest outline of what has happened, and ask him to call Pam at the hospital that evening when we will return for regular visiting hours. I also call her godfather, John, who assists Helena, and ask him to call Pam. He affirms his willingness to take Pam and me into the house with his family. That evening, after Pam talks with both of them, she tells us with a shrug that she's willing to give the *Daime* a try. That's the best we can hope for now.

❧

The next day the hospital calls, saying that our insurance will probably cover a few weeks' stay for Pam. We've talked to the staff and we all agree that Pam needs at least a couple of weeks for full detox and emergency therapy. After a few weeks we'll have Tom put her on a plane home. Then I'll take her to John and Anne's house, where I will live with her for a while until we get clear whether she and the *Daime* community there are a good fit.

It seems like a workable plan.

Except that it isn't life's plan; it's only my mind once again trying to figure things out and take charge. On Tuesday afternoon we get a call from the insurance company saying they will *not* pay anything toward Pam's hospital stay, and that the fees for which we will be responsible are $1,000 a day. At that rate, we can't afford to have her in the hospital for another minute!

In my mind there is now only one option: immediately take her to the *Daime* church and community. John and Anne have two small children, and they are open to having Pam help with them. Pam will have the opportunity to share some responsibility and do weekly *Daime* ceremonies. Donovan is pessimistic but has no better idea. We tell Pam she'll be leaving with us the next day and going to the community. She is accepting but unenthusiastic.

The next morning the lawyer gets the court to rescind the order making Pam a ward of the state so she can be taken out of Nebraska. The psychiatrist gives the order allowing Pam's release from the hospital. By noon we are at the hospital, having said good-bye to Tom and his wife, ready to pick up Pam. On the advice of the psychologist, I make sure the back doors of the car are secure against her opening them during our ride to the airport. We have lunch at the Omaha airport, watchful at all times.

Once in the airport back east, we have a tense parting. Donovan will drive back to our home, and Pam and I will join John and Anne to begin a new life in their *Santo Daime* community.

❧

Pam and I live together in the basement room of the house where John, Anne, their two young children, and two other women from the church reside. For the first few nights Pam suffers from insomnia and nightmares. I stay up with her and listen as she tells me her fears and her bad dreams. I comfort and reassure her as best I can, as therapist, companion, and mom.

When the weekend comes we do our first *Daime* work together. She dresses in the modest all-white clothes required for the ceremony and comes prepared with the appropriate hymnbooks. Mark and many others in the community warmly welcome and embrace her. They seem genuinely pleased that she has come back to the church, and they reassure her that they will be there for her.

I feel in Pam both her childish wanting to be the center of everyone's attention and her deep courage to seek her healing in the *Daime*. Almost as soon as the work begins, she lies down, saying she feels very sick. She vomits a few times but does not complain. She ends the work singing and dancing with everyone.

In May Pam turns eighteen, and the church members hold a special ceremony for her. Our friend Mary Janet receives a hymn[1], in Portuguese, for Pam.

---

[1] As noted before, the teachings in this church are contained in songs which are believed to be received from the spirit world. In Mary Janet's case she woke up in the middle of the night and heard the complete hymn, as if it were being sung to her by Pad. Sebastião, a deceased leader of the church. She sang the hymn into a tape recorder, then went back to sleep. She awoke unable to remember the words or tune until she listened to the recording. This kind of story is not unusual among *Daime* members.

Eu Sei (I Know)

Eu sei que tu tens doenças	I know you have sicknesses.
Pelas tuas doenças tu vais chegar	Through your sickness you are going to arrive.
É com fé e com firmeza	Through faith and firmness
Neste caminho tu vais chegar	On this path you are going to arrive.
Sei que tu já sofreu muito	I know you have already suffered.
Agora sofrendo tu vais chegar	Now through suffering you are going to arrive.
Com a proteção dos anjos	With the protection of angels
A Virgem Mae vai te ajudar	The Virgin Mother will help you.
Sei que tu tas enrolada	I know you are all tangled up
Desenrolando tu vais chegar	Disentangling yourself you are going to arrive
Com humildade e com coragem	With humility and with courage
Com certeza tu vais chegar	With certainty you are going to arrive.
Eu sei que tu esmoreceu	I know you have lost heart.
Eu te dou a luz do alento	I give you the light of courage.
Sei que tu es uma estrela	I know you are a star
Que vai brilhar no firmamento	Which is going to shine in the firmament.

This hymn teaches that by seeing and going through our sickness, suffering, and discouragement with humility and with courage, we can arrive at wisdom and freedom.

At the end of her birthday work Pam wants to go out with some of the young people of the church, and I'm nervous. Now that she's eighteen, I'm anxious that she'll run to the streets again. When I share my concern, Pam confronts me, "Mom, if I wanted to run away and do drugs, I would do it. I know how to find the people who use. It's easy. You couldn't stop me. I'm here because I want to be here. And I'll be here as long as—and only as long as—I want to be here. You can't control my staying or my leaving." She's right, of course. I humbly accept her truth.

Pam behaves herself. During the days she helps with the housework and helps care for the children, nine-year-old Luke and four-year-old Kelly. With them she feels she is reclaiming some of her lost innocence. Every day she listens to tapes of the hymns of the *Santo Daime*, learning the words and melodies. Since the hymns contain the "doctrine" of this church, studying the hymns is comparable to a rabbinical student studying the Torah, or a Buddhist studying the sutras. She attends church ceremonies once a week, dressed appropriately and sitting for extended periods praying or singing hymns. The *Daime* community is rallying to support her, and we are all optimistic about her healing.

✉

Some Brazilian *Daime* leaders who live in the Amazon rainforest community of Mapiá—headquarters of this particular line of the *Santo Daime* religion—come to visit, along with their teenage children. I notice Pam flirting with two Brazilian boys about age fourteen, who are immediately entranced. She changes into a provocative outfit and then invites them to walk with her into the woods out back. I can hardly believe her blatantly seductive, totally inappropriate behavior.

She's out the door with one arm around each boy when Helena spots her and the boys. She sprints over to them and commands, "You all need to go back into the house *now*. Pam, please go in and change your clothes."

"I can dress however I want to dress!" Pam protests. "No one here is the boss of me!"

"Pam," Helena says calmly, "You came to us for healing. You know that your clothes are provocative. You're on dangerous ground here. Do you want your healing or not? We can't keep you here if you're going to act this way with our visitors."

I join Helena and Pam. The boys slink back to the house, and seeing that Helena is serious, Pam is subdued. She seems to snap back into herself, then sputters defensively, "I can't help it. It's just what I do."

Helena probes, "But are you *aware* of what you're doing? Don't you see that these boys are just kids, and they're our guests here. There's no way they could say no to you, but their parents would be really upset."

Pam reluctantly agrees. "I don't know, maybe you're right."

I ask, "Pam, what's up? You told me you wanted to stop this kind of behavior."

"I don't know, Mom, I guess I'm out of control or something… It's like something just takes charge of me, like a power rush to get a guy to look at me like that, to want me. Then all I want is to *get* him. Once it starts I can't stop it. It's weird, like I go far away and this thing just takes over." As the words rush out, she's shaking and starting to cry.

I don't think she's making excuses; I think she's telling the truth.

Helena says, "Let's ask the healers from Mapiá to take a look at you, Pam. We need help with whatever demonic energy is possessing you now. I have to tell you, though, that if your behavior doesn't change in this area, you can't stay here. So please take this seriously."

After the consultation, the healers warn us that they are convinced my daughter is possessed by some serious negative entities which are feeding off her wounded sexuality, and are likely to kill her if they are not removed from her… soon.

❧

Within the worldview of the *Daime* church—which is real for me at the time—this is like a terminal diagnosis for Pam.

The original context of using *ayahuasca* was within a primitive animistic setting in which the world is seen as full of spirit beings. Every plant, animal, and human is seen as an outward expression of an inner spiritual reality. Spirits are very real to an *ayahuasca* shaman.

In the shamanic worldview all illness and negativity are considered a sickness of the soul and assumed to originate from negative spirits. Therefore, while herbal medicines may also be administered, the deeper diagnosis and treatment of disease is based on confronting and exorcising negative or suffering spirits, as well as on consulting and sometimes incorporating healing spirits.

While I do not fully embrace the shamanic worldview I strongly suspect that Pamela's primary defense of dissociation—in which her consciousness withdraws from her body to avoid feeling her terror and her pain—creates an inner psychic vacuum. This vacant space might well be attracting negative entities which take possession of the vacated personality. These entities then act out their own negative compulsions without restraint.

I've seen this before: it's like a "pact with the devil" in which a psychically wounded person unconsciously invites possession by a negative entity to compensate for a personal feeling of weakness. The entity brings the illusion of personal power, and enables the person to act out extremely negative behavior while keeping awareness far away from the underlying reality of emotional powerlessness and vulnerability.

It makes sense to me that unless these negative entities are removed first, Pam will not stand a chance of dropping her defensive dissociation, which she will need to do in order to meet her pain and transform her deeper psychological issues.

The *Daime* healers feel Pam needs something more than the

Daime now. She needs the heavy-duty medicine of someone practicing old-style shamanic exorcism to remove the negative entities that are threatening her life. They recommend a shaman they know who lives in a small city located on the southern edge of the vast Brazilian Amazon forest. I'm willing to try anything. We've tried traditional treatment for addiction at the Chapel School, but it didn't work because Pam never trusted anyone there. She trusts the *Daime* and its healers, and seems ready to take their direction. When she can get some distance from her crazy compulsive behavior, she's eager to get free of it. She recognizes that something has acted out through her sexuality for years now, and she's tired of being controlled by it.

I share all this with Donovan, who agrees that we are dealing with a level of destructive, compulsive behavior that goes beyond ordinary psychological solutions. He's glad to hear that Pam herself now sees this as a problem rather than just acting out without awareness of what she's doing. He adds his support for my taking Pam to this Amazonian shaman saying, "As long as you've brought her back to the *Daime*, you might as well go all the way with their recommendation."

So, with Donovan's blessing, and his financial support, Pam and I leave for the heart of the Brazilian Amazon in search of the shaman the *Daime* healers have recommended.

CHAPTER 13

Jungle Exorcism

Rio Branco, Brazil, July – August 1999

PAM and I fly over miles and miles of Brazilian rain forest to the city of Rio Branco on the river Acre.

Rio Branco is the birthplace of the *Santo Daime* religion. Many different lineages of the *Daime* thrive here, each with different leaders and churches. Rio Branco embraces its *Daime* churches, and both a major bus line and several streets are named after the founder of this religion, Master Irineu.

On the plane into Rio Branco, Pam and I chat with a local government official who proudly tells us that he has many friends in the *Daime* church. He invites us to call on him if we have any needs while we are in his city. His response contrasts sharply with the dismissal we have often received from other middle class Brazilians. When I first broached the subject of our participation in the *Daime* church with one of our Pathwork students in Salvador (a woman therapist), she was aghast, "But that's such a primitive religion! The Pathwork is so much more sophisticated." My eyes must have betrayed my shock, because she earnestly added, as if to seal her judgment, "It's from the *jungle!*"

"I'm surprised at your reaction against the *Daime*," I replied. "I thought because the use of the sacrament is fully legal in Brazil, there'd be more tolerance."

"Oh," she countered, "It's legal, but not *cool!*" (In Brazilian Portuguese slang the same word has both meanings, so what she actually said was, "*Sim, é legal, mas não é* **legal!**")

For Pam and me, then, it is a welcome relief to be coming to a place where the *Daime* is honored.

Rio Branco feels like an old Western frontier town on the edge of vast wilderness. It came into being when the Amazon rainforest was the world's primary resource for rubber, and remains a commercial center for latex and Brazil nuts extracted from the forest. It is also a launching site for ecotourism, a centerpiece of the Brazilian government's efforts to preserve the forest. Many of the city's roads are dirt, and during the rainy season many of these are impassable, thick with mud. During the dry season the air is layered in dust from the roads and smoke from fires burning huge tracts of nearby forest.

While the town has a vibrant commercial life, spirituality and religion seem to be its major enterprise. Every block has a church or two. Evangelicals boom their message from storefronts, Catholics quietly say daily mass at the town's cathedral, and healers go into trance during Spiritism meetings. You can find homeopaths and acupuncturists, along with a great variety of esoteric healers from various Amazonian and African traditions.

The town square has a Catholic cathedral—always open for prayer or quiet contemplation—but also a marketplace where one can buy icons of all the African deities (the *orixás*) and of their darker counterparts (the *exús*), as well as icons of the Christian saints. You can buy grains for offering to the *orixás* or chickens to sacrifice to the *exús*. You can buy esoteric books on healing, crystals or incense to raise your vibration, bells to assist in your meditation. You can purchase the colored candles and ribbons needed for a ritual to bring success in love and business, or you can acquire the requisite black candles and black ribbons to execute any hex or curse.

There is total tolerance here for all flavors of spirituality—from the blatantly superstitious, to the conventionally religious, to the higher reaches of mysticism.

❧

Pam and I arrive in the middle of the night and are taken directly to the *Daime* compound where we meet the next day with *Padrinho* (Godfather) Alfredo, the world-wide leader of this *Daime* church community. He is in Rio Branco on his way back to the Mother Church and community of his line of the *Santo Daime,* based in a rural jungle setting on the Mapiá river.

He knows Pam's case; her reputation has preceded our arrival. We ask his advice and he affirms that some cases need exorcism by a trained shaman. *Padrinho* has heard of the healer/shaman recommended by the healers we'd consulted. He's a man named Antônio who grew up in the *Daime* church, but now practices the African pre-Christian path of *Candomblé.*

I'm wondering how I'm going to find this shaman in a town I don't know and where virtually no one speaks English. And then I remember: I know someone who lives here! Back in the *Santo Daime* community in Mauá, when I was negotiating to buy our little shack there, a Brazilian man visiting that community was called to translate and we'd made an instant connection. After we returned to live in the States, I'd lost track of José (Zé) Luis. What I know about him is that he's a bilingual doctor who used to live in the jungle community of Mapiá, but who now lives here in the town of Rio Branco. The *Daime* people help me connect with Zé Luis and he then helps me rent a VW bug from a local taxi driver. Now our adventure can begin in earnest.

The first job is to locate Antônio. We drive on a pothole-filled dirt road, passing tin and thatch-roofed shacks supported by poles but without walls, to a *Daime* church called *Barquinha* (the little boat), which is led by Antônio's mother. On this road, where some of the city's poorest people live, sits an immaculate whitewashed church with bright lavender trim. At the entrance to the church compound is a tidy outdoor ceremonial area decorated with ribbon-covered poles from which hang lights and strings of colorful plastic holiday banners. The pristine tile-covered interior of the church has a central altar with statues of numerous saints and pictures of its founder, who was originally a disciple of Master Irineu. Small shrines line the back wall, each with offerings of plastic flowers. St. Francis of Assisi is especially honored here, his statue placed above all the others in the bell tower at the church's entrance.

The head of this church is Francisca (Chica) Gabriel, mother of eleven children, Antônio being her eldest son. She is the principal healer for many poor people of this city, the ceremonial leader of all the church services held twice weekly, and the main practitioner and teacher of mediumship in the church.

With Zé Luis's help we get a message to Antônio that we will wait for him here. I notice in passing that none of the boys in the church come near Pam; I assume this is because she radiates a dangerous sexuality. When she can't interest any boys in flirting with her, she withdraws, bored.

When Antônio arrives, Pam perks up. He is handsome, in his forties, laid back and self-possessed. He has the dark skin of a *caboclo*, someone native to the Amazon. He works in construction and is also an instructor of *capoeira*, a Brazilian martial art. Antônio impresses me as smart, self-confident, and at ease.

Pam whispers to me, "He's cool." While Zé Luis and I attend a prayer service in the church, Antônio and Pam hang out in front, smoking cigarettes together and joking in Portuguese. When I return I can see that he's made an alliance with her.

We've come all this way to find this son of the rainforest, who's spent his entire life immersed in the spiritual soup of his Amazonian culture, for a very specific skill he has developed. He practices an ancient shamanic art that some might call witchcraft or voodoo. Since he was raised in the *Daime* church he's at ease with the full range of spirit beings—from recently departed souls, to mischievous trickster spirits, to seriously demonic entities and to ascended Masters—all of which can show up in *Daime* ceremonies.

As a young adult Antônio discovered that extremely negative spirits were attracted to him. He could see devil spirits with his inner eye, and dialogue with them, without being taken over by them. He knew how to keep his center and still interact with them; they respected him and he respected them.

He then studied the African *Candomblé* tradition, which taught him how to deal effectively with these spirits. Over time, Antônio learned how to extract negative entities that were possessing the souls of tormented human beings. He tells us that he works with many lower level spirits (*exús*), which cooperate with him in healing the heavy, dark energies of such people. He further claims to have many *exús* under his command.[1] Here is a man, perhaps unique on the planet, who works respectfully with the very entities that threaten to destroy Pam. He believes he can make contact with those entities and request them to leave her. It's worth a shot.

✸

---

[1] The Afro-Brazilian religions encourage contact with a daunting array of spirit beings—including the many African *orixás* and *exús*—all inter-connected within complex hierarchies and also related to the Catholic pantheon of saints and spirits. I was introduced to this esoteric healing system through contact with Antônio and with the Barquinha *Santo Daime* church. Though I was not drawn to pursue this path, I learned to enter its unfamiliar territory with openness, respect and curiosity.

First Antônio does a diagnostic session with Pam in the living room of his comfortable house, using the *buzios,* African cowry shells that are thrown to create patterns which reveal the issues of his patient. Then we go into town and buy many items needed for the coming ceremonies. Pam is serious and cooperative; she's convinced that she is possessed by negative spirits and she wants to get free. She respects Antônio and comments on the personal power he emanates.

We buy the requisite food and cloth, and he takes us to a small clearing in a forest for Pam's first ceremony. As she stands on the cloth, Antônio and his wife Marilene, his ceremonial assistant, begin chanting. They rub her clothing with three trays of cooked food—corn beans, and flour, each of which his wife has prepared for the occasion. Then they roll candles over her body, which drop onto the cloth along with the food. Finally, a live chicken is rubbed over Pam's body. At his instruction, Pam looks directly into the chicken's eyes and spits three times into its mouth while making prayers to be rid of the devils that possess her. The food is left as an offering for the devils so they will consent to leave her alone, and the chicken is let loose in the woods. She leaves the place of the ceremony, tears streaming, following his instructions not to look back.

Antônio gives her certain prayers to say daily as part of her healing. He also instructs her to have no alcohol, marijuana, or sex during the period of these three ceremonies. She follows his instructions to the letter. I sense that his religion, devoid as it is of any moral judgment, without a hint of Christian or middle-class self-righteousness, fits well with Pam. She starts wrapping her head in a white cloth, unaware that she is imitating the style of *Candomblé* women. Both Antônio and Marilene say they sense she belongs in their line. Pam tells me that if she hadn't found the *Daime* first, she'd want to join them.

The second ceremony is very similar except that the principal food is a fish. The final ceremony for Pam is held all night in the room where we are staying within the *Daime* compound. I am not allowed to be present for this work, though I can hear the chanting and occasional clapping and drumming. She is to sleep with certain foods strapped to her head and others in bowls on the floor around her. Antônio returns early the next morning to complete this work and take the food back as an offering to the *exús*.

For a final work, designed for the two of us, we drive out to his house. I have only seen the dining room where he threw the *buzios*, and the typical front room containing a couch covered in plastic, a few chairs, and a TV. Framed family photos and conventional religious pictures adorn the walls.

He leads us down to a lower level, through the kitchen, and out the back door. Stepping out into his backyard, we enter a different world. Scattered around the yard are tiny buildings that look like miniature doghouses. Each one is the house of a particular *exú* that is under Antônio's command. There are offerings of food and chicken parts in each one. Near the back door of the kitchen is a display of his ritual equipment, including a large metal tray with something that looks like a candelabra on top. He tells me that the blood of sacrificed chickens is dripped onto this altar tray.

Indeed, this final work will be the sacrifice of not one but two chickens—one for Pam and one for me—to be completed here in the backyard. At first I am scared to be involved in this ancient practice of animal sacrifice. I look up at the waxing moon and feel the presence of the universal Mother, the ancient goddess of the first religions on earth, when animal sacrifice was still practiced. I feel her blessing the ritual.

Antônio holds each chicken in front of our faces and asks us to look into its eyes and make our prayers (*pedidos*, requests) before the sacrifice. We are to ask that the negativity that bedevils us be removed. I pray for relief from my anxiety and my self-will. I also pray for Pam to be liberated from the negative forces that have enslaved her. I pray that Pam and I might each find our own way to serve the universal spirit of the Great Mother, whatever that might look like for each of us. While praying, I look directly at the chicken.

And the chicken looks back at me. I feel its consciousness, its aliveness, fully present in this moment. I feel within me a deep honoring of the spirit of this being, and sense its willingness to make the sacrifice. I am grateful.

Calmly, Antônio slits the neck of each of the chickens. Continuing his chants, he squeezes out the blood onto the altar tray. He cuts off the head, legs, feet and wings and arranges them on the tray, which he carries deep into his backyard.

When I later express to Antônio that I feel bad for taking the life of the chicken, he looks straight at me and says, "I know what I'm doing. This chicken's death is honorable, a sacrifice so Pam may not die on the streets from a drug overdose." After that I keep my mouth shut.

Bizarre as these ceremonies seem to my North American consciousness, I notice that after each one Pam is saner, more centered. What is immediately obvious is that the boys both at the *Daime* compound and at the *Barquinha* church are now friendly with Pam, and she is at ease with them without needing to flirt or seduce. She tells me she feels much lighter, more herself, no longer controlled by her compulsion to seduce. Pam also goes out dancing with the teenaged children of Antônio and Marilene and they have good, clean fun, something she hasn't been able to do before.

During our last meeting with Antônio, he tells me privately that there's one catch: His work will only "hold" for about three or four months, he says, after which she will need a refresher. I tell him we can't afford to return that soon to Rio Branco. I am also suspicious: is this just his way to keep making money from Americans? But I choose to ignore my suspicions and concentrate instead on the obvious positive changes I see in Pam.

On our flight back to the States I chuckle ruefully to myself that the only two kinds of work that have so far ever helped Pam—the

Daime and *Candomblé*—are both of dubious legality in the United States, a country that prides itself on its freedom of religion.[2]

---

[2] The status of the *Santo Daime* church has been clarified since that time. In 2006 the Supreme Court of the United States issued a unanimous decision upholding the constitutional right of religious freedom of another Brazilian church (UDV) to use *ayahuasca* as its church sacrament in the U.S. A judge has concluded that this decision sets a clear precedent for a similar case of the *Santo Daime* church in the U.S.

CHAPTER 14

Finding the Good Again

Washington, D.C., August 1999 – March 2000

IN our first *Daime* ceremony back in the States, Pam has a vision of herself inviting men's attention. Then she watches as these men come toward her with knives, intent on slashing her. She senses these bad men are at the door of the room now, and she is frightened that the spiritual power of the group will not be sufficient to deter them from coming in and harming her.

She curls up on her side on the floor, in a fetal position, sobbing with pain. "Help me," she cries out loud. Several of us gather around her as she whimpers, "I just want to die."

Helena comes to Pam and helps her uncurl her body into a more open position lying on her back and then prays over her. Pam says she feels something good enter her, and, gradually, she is able to relax in the presence of this goodness. Later she says she is beginning to understand the teaching behind this terrible vision: that her attraction to flirting and casual sex has really been a kind of torture, a self-mutilation.

The next day Pam, little Kelly, and I take a walk to get an ice cream cone. Kelly says, "Last night when you all went to the work I had a dream that some men with knives were coming after me and Pamela, and I woke up very scared and screaming." Then she adds, "But I knew my big sister Pam would protect me." Kelly's innocent trust of her "big sister" as her protector further bolsters Pam's resolve to keep meeting her fears of the darkness within her that is so graphically revealed in the *Daime* works.

In the next work, Pam experiences the spirit of Ricardo, her Brazilian *favela*-dwelling boyfriend and cocaine dealer, coming to her. She feels as though he has died and is now in spirit form. He is suffering horribly, but also trying to entice Pam back into the kind of life he lived. She is able to stay with herself and say clearly to him, "No, I don't want that life—I want only peace." But she is still scared of him and remembers, "I learned a lot of evil things from Ricardo." She sobs, remembering Ricardo's cruelty to children during the brief time they were together in Salvador.

Suddenly Pam screams and flails on the mattress where she is lying. Her stomach knots and she curls into a ball. Again Helena comes to minister to her. Pam prays that Ricardo will leave her alone, then says to Helena, "Please help me. I'm all tangled up with all these bad things I learned and saw. I need to find the good inside me again." As Helena prays over her, Pam begins to sense the presence of Christ. She weeps as she is washed with waves of light, bringing forgiveness.

During this work, I feel clear, open, and calm. My mind is still and receptive during the *Concentração* (quiet meditation) part of the work, and I feel aligned with spiritual service should anything wish to be done through me. Then, while we are singing a hymn about confronting evil, I have my own *miração* (vision), in the form of a visitation from the spirit of Ricardo. I sense he is trying to get back to Pam. Grounded in my firmness, I evoke a strong protective force field around Pam. I feel absolutely fierce in my defense of her. As the *miração* continues, Ricardo changes from a person to a pure devil—charred flesh, gaping eyes, long claws—determined to wreak destruction.

As I inwardly focus attention on this devil spirit, it begins to dissolve and I see a little boy, desperate for attention and love, frail and suffering. He asks for my help; he wants to hold my hand. I know it is important that I continue to sing the hymns. As I'm singing, I "see" the energy of the hymns creating a kind of handrail for Ricardo, leading from the outer edges of the circle to the altar table in the center of the room. I direct the Ricardo spirit to hold and follow this handrail to the cross at the center of the altar. I see him moving, following the outline of the hymns toward the light-filled altar table. I also see his fear of the light. His identity has been so wrapped up with the dark side that he is afraid he will dissolve in the light, ceasing to exist.

Nonetheless he arrives at the table and prostrates himself in front of the cross, then begins to confess his sins. I see with my inner eyes a dark green-black bile flowing from his mouth that is absorbed by Jesus on the cross. The hand of Christ reaches down to him with utmost tenderness. Ricardo is in tears, overcome with guilt and grief, a wrenching remorse and grief for a life with no real love, no real parenting. The pain is so strong that I, too, am crying. It is good to be able to help another soul to absorb the pain, too intense for any one soul to contain. Ricardo rests at the foot of the cross for the duration of the work. Prayers for the healing of this suffering spirit flow through me.

After this work Pam is never again bothered by the spirit of Ricardo.

ᔐ

I have now been with Pam steadily for several months, during which she has followed all the ceremonial rules in Helena's church and in Antônio's shamanic rituals. She has bravely faced terrible pain and learned how she has brought some of it on herself. She is really doing her inner work.

In Pam's words:
> I remember many works where I wanted to die. A common experience for me was to have a hard time breathing, often catching my breath. This was always very scary for me. I became very

self-conscious during works which made it hard to go inside. But I also knew that I needed to keep showing up because this was a divine being of light that I was fortunate enough to have been allowed to have in my life. Not everybody gets this opportunity. I believed then and will always believe that the *Daime* is a true blessing and no matter what the situation or sickness, it will always do what is best. In my case, it brought the demons to the surface to be exposed and healed.

She drinks the *Daime* even when she is afraid and even when she is nauseated, in faith that healing is arriving. She accepts the frequent purgings and painful feelings that come during the works. Outside of works, she studies the words of the hymns and practices singing them daily. The *Daime* community is rallying to support her; she has someone with her almost all the time.

🙰

Now it's time for me to return to my life with Donovan. Walking up the sidewalk to our beautiful house in the forest, I have the strangest sensation that my feet are not touching the ground. It's as if my consciousness is independent of this body. As this disembodied being, I am fond of this body, as I am fond of my house, but without much attachment to either. The particular life of this particular person is not who I really am at this moment. I am glimpsing the immortal presence that is always and already here, not dependent on form.

Donovan graciously praises me for my faith and perseverance in bringing Pam back to the *Daime* and my courage in taking her for shamanic healing in the jungle. He has been surprised and delighted by Pam's cooperation and healing. It's such a relief for us to be back in loving connection.

We have some wonderfully sweet lovemaking. I discover that,

quite unexpectedly, when I committed to following my inner truth in going to Omaha to bring Pam back to the *Daime* and then taking her to Rio Branco, something deep opened within me, not just spiritually but sexually as well.

We spend the day together at a nearby river. After two days of rain, the air is clear and sparkling, bright white clouds against turquoise blue sky. Lying on the riverbank, we settle into the tall grasses amid wild orange daylilies, caressing each other, relaxing fully into the moment. We enter into the grace of doing nothing, opening fully, letting the presence of being fill up the space—manifesting as breath, clouds, sky, squishy grasses beneath us, fingers gently caressing faces. Contentment.

I have an impulse to enter the river. I cross over a fallen tree trunk and step onto a large flat rock. I dip my feet into the water and discover it's not as cold as I expected. Upstream I see the calm reflections of leafy trees; downstream are choppy, darker water and rock outcroppings. This place is an extension of the rocky shore, where the river hurries over in small waterfalls. I pick my way to the center of the rocks and lie down in this small bed created by rocks and water.

Closing my eyes as the water rushes into my crown chakra and then divides into two streams that wash down each side of my body, I feel that the water is washing my sins away. I am being restored to the innocence of knowing what I know, of being what I am, of seeing with the clear eyes of love. Donovan joins me in the river and we embrace, holding on to each other and receiving the water's cleansing.

§▲

For many months after my return home to Donovan and my work, I travel to the *Daime* community at least two days every week to join them in ceremony and spend time with Pam. She is still receiving much healing from the *Daime* and seems content with her life in the community. She loves spending time with Luke and Kelly, and their parents say that Pam is fitting in well. She takes the preliminary GED test and does well; she is confident she can pass it and get her high school equivalency degree.

She's apprehensive about learning to drive, so we don't push her. But she gets a job! She works in a day care center located in a local woman's home, mostly taking care of infants. Her employer is very pleased with her work. People in the church have to drive her there and back; I drive her to and from her work when I'm there for my weekly visit.

Donovan joins me on the special occasion of a *Daime* work led by *Padrinho* Alfredo, the Brazilian leader of the *Daime* worldwide church. It is the first time Donovan has seen Pam since their tense parting at the airport several months earlier. It will be a celebratory dancing work.

Tonight is a special night for our family because it marks the moment when Pam will become an initiate of the church, comparable to the ceremony of adult baptism in some churches. In this ceremony the new initiate is given a silver star, symbolic of the bright spiritual essence in each of us, which will be worn at all subsequent *Daime* ceremonies.

Pam and I and several of the young Brazilian women go to the bathroom to make final adjustments to the white outfit Pam is wearing. I take photos of her dressing as if this were her wedding—maybe it is.

Padrinho Alfredo calls Pam to the center of the group, embracing and congratulating her. Helena comes forward and pins the star on Pam's blouse. Helena calls me and Donovan to the center and takes pictures of the three of us together. Pam reaches up to give Donovan a kiss. I feel some melting between them.

Pam speaks in Portuguese to those around her, saying this is the most *lindo* (beautiful), *maravilhoso* (marvelous) moment of her life.

Padrinho Alfredo speaks to Pam: "You are now seriously entering school—the school of self-knowledge, a mystery school. You are on a path for meeting God. Your parents can be proud of you for taking on the challenge of entering this school. You will learn much. I pray you may become an inspiration for other young people in trouble to seek their healing through the *Daime*."

Padrinho's words will come back to me often as I struggle with how to explain to others what she is doing, how to justify continuing to support her financially. I can affirm that she is in a serious mystery school. If she were in college, we would not hesitate to support her. Is what she is doing now less important than college? No. It is just as important, and I need to stand by her and by that truth.

After the work, Pam is very sweet and open. She says, "I know that sometimes I push you away, and that isn't right. I'm sorry. I know you are my mother, my true mother, who has always taken care of me. I'm very grateful. Thank you so much."

It is a stunning recognition of the deep bond that is now growing solid between us, grown to fullness since the rescue in Omaha. The bonding that didn't happen with her biological mother at birth, and still didn't happen with me during her fifteen years of living with us, is now evident to us both.

ॐ

Nine months after our arrival at this *Daime* community, Helena is diagnosed with colon cancer. Even though she continues to lead all the works, it's clear that she's sick and getting sicker. People in the community are upset, and there is much fear about the future. The spiritual container for Pam's healing suddenly feels shaky.

We are uncertain what to do about Pam. The people who have been driving her to her day care job can no longer afford the time, and so she loses her job. She keeps putting off taking her GED exam. John, her godfather, reports that she's behaving somewhat erratically and staying out at night later than her curfew. After he discovers some beer bottles in her bedroom trash, we have a meeting together with Helena. Pam says she wants to stay in the church house and work it out.

I remember Antônio's caution that his work would only hold for about three or four months. It's now been seven months since we visited him, and two months since Helena's serious diagnosis. Pam is definitely slipping.

Two days after our meeting with Helena and John, in early March 2000, eleven months after Pam and I arrived in this *Daime* community, John calls to say that Pam has gone. He has no idea where she is.

CHAPTER 15

Through the Door of Devastation

Rio Branco, Brazil, March – April 2000

FOR two days Pamela calls no one. Then she telephones me to say not to worry about her because she has a great job "escorting" and has "friends" she can stay with near Dupont Circle in Washington, D.C.—an area of the city where young people go to party. I'm speechless. She is almost nineteen years old; is this really the life she's choosing? She won't tell me where she's living and doesn't want to see me. It's now been almost a year since the rescue in Omaha. Since then, she has lived a decent life in a serious spiritual community—but now she's gone. Again.

I am scheduled to teach in Brazil three days from now. I have no idea how I will be able to do it. The day of my night flight to São Paulo, I am at my ninety-two-year-old mother's house, sobbing uncontrollably. My mother is ready to call 911. All she can imagine is that I must be having a heart attack—and I am, but of a nonphysical kind.

On the ride to the airport everything passes in slow motion and nothing feels quite real. As I wait for the plane, I pull out the only book I've brought with me, about a man's personal spiritual journey to no-self, to the awakened state.[1] Reading this book is the only thing that

---

[1] *The Journey to No-Self: A Personal Account of the Mystical Experience*, by Patrick Drysdale. This was one of the first books by a contemporary awakened Western man about his journey. Now there are such books by many others—Eckhart Tolle, Adyashanti, Gangaji, and Byron Katie among them.

keeps me sane. I read:

> It became obvious that what I called "my" life was nothing
> but a series of impersonal events. It was an unsettling surprise
> to see that all the nervousness and anxiety in the past was a big
> waste of energy because, in reality, there wasn't any me for "my"
> life to belong to.... I understood more deeply than ever that I
> didn't have to push the river of life. It flowed all by itself.
>
> Since it was all God's doing anyway, I learned to accept
> every situation that came along and lived with a calm indiffer-
> ence to what transpired in my life. The self that worried about
> what might happen had disappeared and the old nature was
> no longer there to feel afraid.

The possibility of this state of consciousness calls to me, but "calm
indifference to what transpires in my life" seems unimaginable. Still,
something inside me knows the state being described is real—and is,
indeed, my destiny.

Every day of working in Brazil, I help people do their personal
psychological work—to open the numb places, let the feelings flow,
uncover the misconceptions formed in childhood that govern their
lives. Every evening after teaching, I flee to my room and seek solace
in this book that illustrates a new way to be with experience: neither
being whipped around by all the ups and downs of life, nor being in
denial. Instead the author is pointing to true detachment that can only
come from letting go in total trust of a greater reality. I know that only
this larger perspective will allow me to survive the fear and grief that
threaten to overwhelm me. I read and reread the author's story, trying to grasp his awakened perspective. I cannot understand it, nor can
my mind relax from what is troubling me, but somehow just being
reminded that such a perspective exists brings some calm.

ॐ

At the end of my teaching, I meet my friend Barbara at the São Paulo airport. Together we travel to Rio Branco. I want to explore this unusual city for myself.

In my first time here with Pam, we had participated in many *Daime* ceremonies both at the *Daime* compound and at the *Barquinha* church, in addition to attending the rituals with Antônio. On my last day I had visited the tomb of Master Irineu, founder of the *Daime* church.

Raimundo Irineu Serra was a very tall black man from the mostly Afro-Brazilian northeast part of Brazil, where he was raised by a devoutly Catholic mother. In the 1920s, he moved to the state of Acre to work as a border guard (Brazil borders both Peru and Bolivia here). He learned the use of *ayahuasca* from Peruvian Indian shamans, then started drinking the sacrament on his own.

He received a vision of the Divine Mother in the moon. She became his teacher and guide, teaching him prayers to say and hymns to sing. These prayers and hymns became the basis for his starting a new path, which evolved into the church of the *Santo Daime*. He came to be known as Master Irineu, and was well-respected in Rio Branco. His congregation included many former alcoholics, and several people who were cured of terminal illness. He was known far and wide in this Amazon town as a remarkable healer and spiritual teacher. Master Irineu had an abiding connection to the Divine Mother and a deep awakening to his spiritual nature.

Though he died in 1971, those who drink *Daime* frequently feel that his spirit visits them during the works. When he first came to me in a *miração* in Mauá, I recognized Master Irineu as my next spiritual teacher. His presence aroused in me the same awe and inspiration I had felt in the early 1960s in the presence of my first spiritual teacher, Reverend Martin Luther King, whose teachings of liberation and non-violence were a guiding light for me. For a while in my young adulthood I was immersed in the civil rights struggle and in an African-American culture which I found deeply nourishing—forgiving, heart-centered and faith-filled. It was during this time that I opened my heart to the inner-city black street kid Christopher, who became my godson.

In meeting the Afro-Brazilian spiritual teacher Master Irineu—through drinking *Daime*—I felt like I was coming home to a deeply familiar place in my soul.

Master Irineu's open-air tomb in Rio Branco is a place of reverence for anyone who drinks *Daime*. When I first visited here, I felt overwhelmed by the spiritual presence and power I felt—and I had taken no sacrament that day.

This pristine outdoor sanctuary feels like my true church. The tomb is located on a stretch of unpaved country road on the outskirts of the city, across from M. Irineu's original *Alto Santo* church, which is now led by his widow. The grounds around both the whitewashed church and the blue-tiled tomb are beautifully maintained with carefully tended jungle vegetation and bounteous flowers. Outside is a sign requesting appropriate clothing, the removal of shoes, and silence in the tomb. Inside is the raised sarcophagus of the founder. The interior of the building, with its waist-high walls, is covered in light-blue tile.

The tomb is a sanctuary for many ordinary townspeople who come here to pray, light candles, say a rosary, leave plastic flowers, or just touch the Master's final resting place. Simple, devout people come here every day, everyone in silent reverence for the magic of this place. I too have been led to this spot.

After my first trip to the tomb, I wrote in my journal:

> *I know I am a flower in the Master's garden. His tomb is the most soothing place I have ever been; my body and soul resonate in complete harmony with the vibration here. I feel an immense serenity—a calm that permeates into the bone marrow, a peace*

that dissolves coagulated pockets of fear, letting them melt back into a continuous flow of love. I feel the Master's presence intimately. We talk. I feel my devotion to him. He keeps bringing me back to friendship and mutual respect. He is immensely reassuring, humble, respectful. I know myself as part of his team, another star orbiting his brilliance.

Though I knew I needed to come back to this place, I did not know how desperately I would need what could be found here. By the time Barbara and I arrive in Rio Branco to our sparsely furnished room in the *Daime* hostel, I am emotionally and physically exhausted.

🜲

Barbara and I go to the tomb at least once each day for two weeks, often starting with a short morning service of saying prayers and singing some of the hymns of Master Irineu at six a.m., which is sunrise pretty much year round this close to the equator. We are always alone in the early morning, and after we sing we sit in silence, opening to the new day, letting in the sounds of birds and bugs, sensing the spiritual presence here—and in my case letting the pain of recent disappointments wash over me.

It is clear that the time has come for my own healing. The many shocks and wounds I've experienced in mothering Pamela have taken their toll on my body. I feel deflated, defeated, a failure. Like Job in the Old Testament story, I have exhausted my efforts to understand. I accept that no explanation will ease the simple pain of heartbreak.

I need to sit with the exhaustion and the defeat without trying to evaluate or analyze or question anything. I need space and time to let the pain be, just as it is. And this is my sacred space where I know all will be received, all will be held.

Inside my body are grief, fear, and confusion. All this comes to the surface for recognition and release. I cry and pray and allow whatever needs to come up to flood to the surface. And when my tears subside, I rest in the hollow emptiness that is all that remains. My body becomes a vast, raw tenderness. Into this vulnerable tissue I let in the strength and love that surround me in this place. The tomb becomes the holy place where I can let myself die. All my expectations, hopes, and dreams come to the surface and shatter. I do this day after day until I finally land somewhere near the bottom.

❦

One morning Barbara and I drink some *Daime* in an early-morning ceremony at the hostel where we are staying. We are still feeling its effects when we arrive at the tomb. I'm unusually raw and needy on this day; my singing is interrupted with the sound of my own voice crying softly. My mind is empty.

In the silence following our singing, I start regressing in my consciousness to the feeling state of an infant. I feel lost and, most of all, bereft. Where is my mother? *Where is my mother?* **Where is my mother?** I can feel the infant frantically scanning, screaming, searching for the single most important presence in her life... and there is nothing. The loss stabs deep into my heart as my belly clenches, and I double over.

I have done lots of regression work in the past, but this is different and deeper. It's personal, but beyond the personal. It's a universal feeling of loss and disconnection. Sharp, serrated pain cuts through my body, reaches into all the deepest recesses, and scrapes out every bit of scabbed-over disappointment and loss. Slowly and of its own accord, the pain lets go.

I feel washed clean, more empty than ever before in my life. But now it is a quiet emptiness, an emptiness that lacks nothing.

⚘

Throughout our time in Rio Branco Barbara has been steadfast and patient with me—simply receiving and supporting me, not trying to fix or change what needs to well up in its own way. I am immensely grateful for her support.

She has also helped me enjoy this unusual place. We take daily walks in a park filled with old jungle trees with plaques naming each one. We watch for unusual birds and hang out in the city's central square with the food carts and musicians, eating the mangoes that are so plentiful they rot in the gutters. We get our food from the open air market, including our daily drink of *açaí* juice, long before it would become a health food fad. We cook in the communal kitchen at the *Daime* hostel, for ourselves and for the other *Daimistas,* Brazilian and foreign, who pass through here on their journey deeper into the rainforest to the *Daime* spiritual community of Mapiá.

Or we eat at the *por kilo* restaurants where we pay according to what the food weighs. We visit my doctor friend Zé Luis, and along with him, we do *Daime* ceremonies at several different churches. We enjoy exploring all Rio Branco has to offer. But nothing touches me nearly as deeply as my time in Master Irineu's tomb.

At the end of the two weeks Barbara has to fly back to the States, but I know I need more time here. Donovan agrees that it makes no sense to hurry home. Pam is truly gone—for now at least—and my work can wait. While I am grateful for Barbara's comfort and friendship, I know I need to take my next steps alone.

CHAPTER 16

The Mother and I Are One

Rio Branco, Brazil, April 2000

I CONTINUE my early morning visits to the tomb. Gradually, I feel less pain and more emptiness. The question "Where is my mother?" had welled up from the deepest place in me, the original separation we all experience when we take birth in human form. Slowly, almost imperceptibly, the question is now morphing into something even more basic: "*What* is my mother? *What* am I? Are we really separate?"

These questions begin to gather momentum inside me. I want to break through whatever is holding me back from union with my true nature. I want to meet in myself the feminine face of God. I want to know what life is all about—not just my personal drama, but the whole human drama. I want to know the mystic's reality, the one described in *Journey to No-Self*. I have a sense of an interior intensity that is not only building, but is also taking charge of this life.

Years earlier, in the early 1960s when I was given my first glimpses of the spiritual path, I had a vision of having a rope tied around my waist, connected to a large wheel, a winch. Something un-nameable was turning that winch and drawing me into itself. I sense that now the winch is turning again and I am being dragged to a destiny that I can never understand with my mind.

☙

In a morning ceremony I drink *Daime*, then afterwards go to the tomb to await instruction. I find myself in deep meditation, repeating a kind of mantra: "What is it? What is it?" I can't assign a name to this "it" that I seek, but the urgency of the question is undeniable.

Then the mantra spontaneously ceases, the mind stops altogether, and an emptiness that is vast—not personal, more like cosmic, formless space—opens up inside. As long as I keep my eyes closed, this space grows ever more immense.

As an experiment, I open my eyes. Immediately, the spaciousness crystallizes into all the forms seen around me—blue tiles, green trees, blue sky, this bench, and this body sitting on this bench. I take it all in, all at once, and a "voiceover" announces: *"This is It."*

Everything pulsates with life; I perceive an undulating tapestry of organic life forms that are intricately interconnected. Whatever is animating this gigantic tapestry of life animates every part of it equally, including this body sitting on this bench. No one part of it is more special than any other part—and none of it is personal. Nothing is "mine." There is no identification with any part as separate from the whole. It all comes from the same Source: actually it all *is* the same Source, dressed in myriad forms.

I am enthralled. I find that when my eyes close, there is only the formless vastness. When they open, I am plunged into this exquisitely alive, sparkling fabric of infinitely interconnected forms. Nothing is separate from anything else—and there is no separate "me."

And then more words come: *"The Mother and I are One."*

I have come to know the Divine Mother as my true mother, the spiritual fount from which my individual spirit flows and upon which my life depends. But what is happening now is new. It erases all sense of separation between the Godhead or Source or Mother and this particular body that is still sitting on this particular bench in this exact place at this precise moment. This, too, is God, here and now. There is no "individual spirit"; there is only Her. She is blue sky and blue tiles, green vegetation, and this body and this mind. She is all of it, here and now.

I know that what I am experiencing is the same reality Jesus realized and tried to communicate when he said "the Father and I are One." Or that Buddha pointed to when he said, "In all the universe I am the only One."

Spontaneously the body gets up and starts to move around the tomb, gliding, dancing, delighted. I go out into the surrounding gardens and truly feel that I am in the Garden of Eden, seeing the world as if for the first time. Not separate from what is witnessed, I am completely childlike, innocent, open. The Mother is this garden, this human female, this blue-tiled tomb—we are all Her incredible play, and there is nothing outside it, nothing excluded from it.

And there is no meaning outside of this play; its very existence, its is-ness, *is* the only meaning. It is all Her unfolding, everything exactly as it is: one undulating, animated, and unbounded wholeness. Everything is dancing Her joy.

The sound of traffic reaches the ears, and this body spontaneously turns back toward the tomb. Then something on the ledge of the low wall of the tomb catches attention: a snake. And then the snake explodes into a thousand snakes, and the fear-thought arises that they are all coming off the wall and heading toward me.[1]

Fear sneaks into paradise, and the experience of Oneness shatters. When looking at the proliferation of snakes, this thought is directed to them: "I know you are not real, and I want to see and know only what is true." They retreat back into the one snake that truly is here, which slowly slithers down the wall and away. As I watch, the snake appears

---

[1] This experience of the multiple snakes is the only hallucination I ever experienced in the *Daime*. I have "seen" many spirit forms, but these have a certain reality at the transpersonal level; never before or since have I seen something that was only a projection of my personal fear-mind.

to look back at me and then disappears in the undergrowth.

I cannot fully return to my earlier state. Fear has had its entry point, creating separation between the snake and the witness of the snake.

But I have had an enormous shift of perspective, and will never forget it. Since experiencing it, I have never doubted that my true nature is spirit, identical with the true nature of God (or the Divine Mother). Nor have I doubted that, in essence, all manifestation is only the outer garment of the Divine, all forms reflecting a formless spiritual essence. There is no material "something" with an independent existence. And there is no independent "me."

❧

Much later I would recognize that this experience was a taste of what is often called "awakening" in spiritual literature. It is a universal spiritual experience that mystics of all traditions—Jewish, Muslim, Christian, Buddhist, Hindu, and others—have described. It is essentially the same for everyone, from whatever religious or spiritual background. We open to the reality of what we are as spirit, which is vast and empty and eternally alive as compared to how we normally think about ourselves as a separate limited human body which will die.

Spiritual awakening is comparable to waking up from a nighttime dream and realizing that, while the "character" we were playing in the dream felt very real, it is obviously not the truth of what we are when we wake up. It is a shift of perspective in which we come to know, not as a thought but as a lived experience, that our true nature is one with Source and that this Oneness is the only reality that truly exists.

The thirteenth-century poet Rumi illustrates my journey:

The way of love is not
a subtle argument.

The door there
is devastation.

Birds make great sky-circles
of their freedom.
How do they learn it?

They fall, and falling,
they're given wings.[2]

Following the way of love, I have fallen fully through the door of devastation. I have been given wings. I have glimpsed freedom.

❧

The intense energy of this breakthrough into a deeper level of reality stays with me for several weeks. I barely sleep, and I'm filled with joy.

There are curious manifestations of my new awareness. For instance, I find myself suddenly much more conversant in Portuguese and have conversations with Brazilians I wouldn't previously have thought myself capable of. I also have a newfound confidence in driving my rented VW all over town with *Daime* friends who come through Rio Branco, navigating potholes and washboard roads that would have intimidated me before.

I feel that I possess an incredible secret. I plainly see that most people don't know who they are: divinity itself. I feel greatly comforted in knowing that I will be able to share this experience fully with Donovan.

---

[2] Reprinted by permission of Coleman Barks from *The Essential Rumi*.

When thoughts of Pam arise, at first there is sadness. I want her to know what has been shown to me, and to rest in her inner, infinite worth. But for the first time, I also begin considering the possibility that who she is right now—a young woman choosing to do drugs with other young people and live a precarious existence on the streets of Washington, D.C. —is also an expression of divinity. Allowing myself this perspective gives me relief; I know, at least for now, that what is happening in Pam's life isn't "wrong." It just is what it is. And her life and problems aren't about *me*. Her life is an expression of God the Mother, doing whatever She does, as Pam.

I feel a rush of gratitude to Pam for being exactly who she is: someone who has challenged every particle of my conventional middle-class identity, and every idea I've had about myself as a mother. Because of her I have been plunged into deep self-examination, opening hidden pockets of pain and emerging into a brighter light than I ever dreamed possible. I acknowledge that Pam has been the greatest catalyst for my spiritual growth. At the same time, I release her to her own destiny.

⚘

After my experience in the tomb, I decide to go to Mapiá, a journey I had always considered daunting before. Getting there takes three full days from Rio Branco, first by auto and then by canoe. I travel to Mapiá and back with new Brazilian friends, sharing a canoe ride, sleeping in a hammock covered by mosquito netting in the home of one of the founders of the village, walking alone in the jungle, dealing with the heat and the bugs.

I go to large *Daime* works in the village church and do daily prayer services with my hostess. I even meet with *Padrinho* Alfredo at his mother's house—and we speak Portuguese. Despite my anticipation of an arduous trek, the trip to Mapiá is seamless, flowing, easy.

I particularly enjoy a *Daime* work called a *gira,* which is held outdoors in Padrinho Alfredo's *terreiro* (sacred outdoor sanctuary). I feel well received and spiritually nourished in Mapiá, but I also sense a detachment from the church of the *Santo Daime.*

The reality revealed in the tomb is the basis of my new ease. I have seen beyond the religion of the *Santo Daime* (or any other path or church), recognizing that they are all boats for carrying their followers to the other shore—awakening to our true nature. Once we have been shown what we are, we have a new relationship to the boat which helped us to arrive. In the past I had always tried too hard to be a "good girl," obedient to the many rules and beliefs of this church. My identification with the good girl persona meant twisting myself into something that did not feel natural to me, bringing exhaustion and resistance. Now I feel free of this demand on myself to conform. Ironically, this allows me to be in the works with less rebellion, more harmony with the ceremonial forms, and more enjoyment.

After a life-changing five weeks in Brazil, I return home feeling empowered and relaxed. I am confident that spirit is living this life and it will do whatever is needed to help Pam.

CHAPTER 17

No One Wants To Be an Addict

Washington, D.C., May – August 2000

I COME back from Brazil feeling greater detachment from the drama
of Pam's life. For the first time, the habitual refrain in my mind—
"What will become of her now?"—has a spacious, soothing quality, like
cellos playing in the background. I feel a simple curiosity, an openness to whatever happens.

Pam writes:

> I'm not sure what happened. Maybe it was just time to move
> on. One day I was living in the church house and the next day I
> was in the city, crashing with whoever would have me, drinking
> and smoking pot most days, going to raves[1] or other parties when
> I could.
>
> Probably I got bored with being good. Being in Helena's
> church was all about being good and resisting temptation. I did
> it as long as I could. But when Helena got sick, I started drinking
> an occasional beer with some of the other young people in the
> church. Then it was all over. I'm that kind of addict.

𝕤

---

[1]Raves are all-night dance parties at club venues, fueled by drugs including
Ecstasy and Ketamine.

Pam calls, and we arrange to meet for lunch at a restaurant near Dupont Circle. I'm curious: Will she show? (She does.) Will she be ravenous from malnutrition? (Not apparently.) Will she be on drugs? (Yes, she probably is). But we simply enjoy being together, focusing on the food and on our connection, and I catch her up on the church people and their lives and my adventures in Brazil. I show her my photos from Mapiá. After lunch we sit on the late spring grass in Dupont Circle Park with other drug-using young people while they chainsmoke cigarettes and pass around a brown paper bag concealing a large bottle of beer. They chat about parties they either have attended or are planning to attend. Their lives seem to be all about parties—raves in particular.

Then Pam takes me to where she sleeps: a pillow crammed into a tiny closet in the small apartment of a young gay man who deals drugs. She seems content with her life of party, drugs, casual sex, more parties, and more drugs. In a moment of candor she reveals, "There's lots of rave parties and drugs on the weekends, but then all the kids from the suburbs go home, and only some of us are still left here looking for more."

She says that she feels like she's on vacation from all the hard inner work she did in the church community, surrounded by all those good people who she felt looked down on her. Her party friends don't judge her. She says she needs this break, implying that she might return after she's had enough vacation. My mind wants to latch onto this likely delusion because it offers a more acceptable future, thus making it easier to tolerate what I am witnessing of her present life. Still, when I leave her, I feel okay; I am accepting her reality without trying to change it. This alone feels liberating.

We set up another lunch date; she fails to show. I stop trying to arrange meetings. When I call Pam on her birthday in May, her voice is so slurred from the drugs she's on that I can barely make out her words; it sounds like she's saying something about disappearing into a hole. When I ask if she's in danger, she won't (or can't?) answer and then there's a clattering noise. I assume the receiver has fallen from her hand, or…?

I panic. Is she going mad? Is she being abducted or abused? Should I drive the two hours from my home to Dupont Circle, right now? My sanity returns long enough for me to realize I have no chance of convincing her to stop using drugs.

Repeated calls to that number bring no response. When she finally calls several days later, she casually tells me that she's left that apartment. The guy there accused her of stealing his drugs. She denies it, but who knows? She reveals that the day I called she'd been on Ketamine, an animal tranquilizer so powerful that users refer to its effect as "disappearing down a K-hole."

She tells me she has a new friend named Billy Bob. I assume he's her boyfriend; actually, he's her drug dealer. She's now sleeping on park benches in Dupont Circle, except when she can get a guy to let her share his bed. Her homeless lifestyle makes it clear: This is something very different from a vacation. Billy Bob deals crystal meth amphetamine, and the moment she hooks up with him marks her entry into the realm of life-threatening addictive street drugs.

Pam writes:
> One evening Billy Bob tells me he has a surprise for me and takes me to a downstairs apartment in Dupont Circle, the home of one of his gay friends. He takes me into a back room and shows me a needle full of a clear liquid—crystal meth amphetamine.[2] He says, "This is the real deal. You'll love it." He injects it in my arm and looks up at me. I feel warm, but not much else.

---

[2] Crystal meth-amphetamine is a colorless, powerful and highly addictive chemical stimulant which often leads to obsessive actions.

He says he hasn't given me enough, so he fixes another needle and gives me the shot. My body gets burning hot and my eyes cross. I feel for sure I'm going to die. But it also feels so good. The chemical taste in my mouth makes me cough. He tells me that's how it's supposed to feel. I stay awake for the next week, walking the streets, "geeking" on doing my fingernails, cutting my clothes, and other dumb stuff.

From then on, whenever I did any drug, I would just keep doing more until I felt like I might die. I didn't stop until I felt I might need to get to an emergency room.

Pam becomes addicted not just to crystal meth, but also to her drug dealer:

After a rave I spend all night in a hotel with some rich yuppie guys, and they give me $200. I don't even do anything for it! I go back into D.C. and track down Billy Bob. I give him all the money because I know he can get much more crystal than anyone else for that amount of money.

He tells me to wait on the corner and he will be back when he can. I wait and wait and wait. I hang out right there for six hours. Finally, I give up. I try to hunt him down, but to no avail. The next thing I remember is waking up on a bench in Dupont Circle, with Billy Bob screaming my name. He smiles and tells me to come with him. I forget all about how long it has taken. He always hooks me up, eventually....

I really was infatuated with Billy Bob. What he said, I did, no questions asked, and in his own way he treated me very well and liked me back. Maybe it's difficult for anyone to understand my sentiment for a dealer who just used me, someone so seemingly heartless and cruel. But when you live on the streets, you enter a different world and it is hard to explain the feelings you have for people you meet there. I guess you grab on to whoever you can for even a taste of love, compassion, and understanding.

In short order, Pam is introduced to the other major destructive drug that will control her life for the next few years.

Scotty, a friend of Billy Bob's, introduces me to heroin. I don't have any meth; I need drugs and I could care less what I put in my body if it alters my mind in any way. I have already tried GHB,[3] Special K,[4] and numerous pills that I pop in my mouth as they are given to me, not questioning what they are or what they will do to me. Scotty and I go to his friend's house in Georgetown[5] where Billy Bob and his girlfriend also live.

I am fascinated by the whole scene. Needles, baggies, and drug addicts. I love it. I ask for a bag of heroin and Scotty says fine. I copy them, not really knowing what I am doing. But when it comes to sticking the needle in my vein, I can't fake that. I ask if he will shoot me up. I say I've done it before a lot, but I don't like sticking myself. So he does it for me. At first I feel so warm and good. All emotional pain melts away. It is impossible to feel any bad feelings. No crying, no guilt, nothing. But simple stuff bothers me, like loud music. We go down to 22nd and P Street, to Soho Coffee Shop. The hot spot. The minute I get out of the car I throw up on the sidewalk.

The next day all I want is more. I track Scotty down and tell him I have to have more immediately. He smiles, and that is the beginning of my heroin addiction.

---

[3]GHB is a sedative used as a rave party-scene intoxicant. At high doses it can produce a coma-like sleep.

[4]Special K is Ketamine, the animal tranquilizer.

[5]Georgetown is an upper-middle class area of Washington DC, where Georgetown University is located.

After her first few uses of heroin, Pamela calls me from a phone booth in Georgetown. "I'm freaked out doing heroin. I'm living in a place where everyone is using needles by ten a.m. Billy Bob's girlfriend shoots heroin and works as a stripper. One guy has a downtown job, and he keeps it together. He's been using heroin for years. Others don't do anything but shoot up all day."

I volunteer to come into town and take Pam to a hospital to detox; she declines. I ask if she has clean needles. "Yes, there's a needle exchange place where we can get twenty-five clean needles for four dollars."

For the next several weeks, as her heroin use escalates, she makes frequent calls to me and to her former friends in the *Daime* church, telling us exactly what is happening but refusing help. We learn the general location of the house in Georgetown; we also learn the names of the players and dealers in the heroin-fueled dramas of her life.

She's a racing car whose accelerator is stuck to the floor, yelling out to the hapless spectators lining the course that she's out of control. As our stomachs churn and our hearts burn, we all know she's going to crash. We gasp from the sidelines in horror.

Now spacious curiosity is out the window, which is sealed tight with thick black fear. I can no longer tolerate my suffocating feelings of helplessness. I pick up the phone and contact an organization in D.C. called HIPS (Helping Individual Prostitutes Survive), which does wonderful work to help rescue addicted girls from the streets. I talk to one of their counselors about Pam for over an hour; she is deeply sympathetic.

I also find a private investigator who works for free to locate runaway children; he will help any time I want to locate Pam. I feel tempted to have him find her now and turn her into the police. The PI strongly recommends against this, though, as it will assure her cutting off all contact with me. If she gets arrested, that's great, but I shouldn't be the agent for her arrest.

For me it is a comfort just to know that advice and help exist in D.C. I can accept that for now there is nothing more that either HIPS or the PI can do for me or for Pam, until she wants help.

I also start going more regularly to Al-Anon; at least it's something to do. I struggle to accept Step One: "Admitted we were powerless ..." Facing and accepting my utter helplessness in the face of my daughter's addiction is my greatest challenge. By constantly repeating this first step, every few minutes, my tolerance for feeling powerless grows, if only by nanoseconds.

Pam calls me, saying, "The other night I had cotton fever. It's like a twenty-four-hour flu with chills. You get it from impurities getting through the cotton before shooting the heroin." She also says she's having weird periods lately, including a lot of spotting between cycles. She wants to go to the doctor.

"I will take you to a doctor if you want to get clean," I offer. She declines. I tell her about HIPS and give her the number to talk with a counselor there, but she never calls them.

For the next two weeks Pam calls only to tell me she's alive but doesn't want to see me. Then, suddenly, she does. I now have a cell phone, and she's calling me when I'm already in D.C. for a church work. She's says she's in the Dupont Circle park and promises not to leave until I get there. Later she tells me that her actual plan is to get another hit of heroin before I arrive so she won't be dope-sick (in the throes of heroin withdrawal) when we meet.

I spot her sitting alone on the grass. In slurred words, she mumbles, "I want to get clean." Then she asks for my lipstick. I watch as she smears the red onto her lips and then down onto her chin. Then the lipstick tube drops from her hand, which falls lifeless into her lap. Her head jerks, then droops down to her chest, and she falls asleep. So this is what nodding off on heroin looks like.

I feel oddly calm, comforted by being here, seeing first-hand what it's like for her. As I take her limp hand in mine, love wells up in my heart. I sing a few hymns quietly, and then lapse into silent prayer. About a half hour later she wakes up, agitated and disoriented. I remind her she said she wanted to get clean. "Yes," she says again, "I need to go back to the church." I call some people in the church who are ready to receive her, to let her stay at their house.

As we walk toward my car, she gets agitated again. She keeps glancing toward a coffee shop we're passing on P Street. This is where she scores drugs, she admits, and she feels a strong pull to go in. But she resists and we get to the car.

We drive to the church house; she's already starting to feel achy and irritable. I make calls to treatment centers and learn the basic outline of what's involved in heroin detox. Although it is very painful—cold chills, hot flashes, terrible aches and pains in the joints—it does not usually constitute a medical emergency. (This is unlike detoxification from serious alcoholism, which must be overseen by a doctor because the side effects can be fatal.) I am at her side, getting her fluids (she can't eat), getting her some pain medication from a doctor friend, and offering whatever comfort I can.

She confesses that she loves how heroin makes her feel, but she's very scared of becoming possessed by the drug, the way she used to feel possessed sexually. Most of all, she's scared of losing me. The people in the house are very kind, each coming to her in turn, offering prayers or hymns or a comforting word. They urge her to come back to the church; I want her to go into residential treatment.

At the end of the weekend she's clear that she's not ready for either move; she wants to go back to Georgetown. She tells me, "I have a strong will, Mom, and I don't want to do any more heroin. I just want to go back to my friends." I don't know if she believes what she's saying or not, but I certainly don't. Nonetheless, I take her to a restaurant where she finally eats a weekend's worth of food, and then I drop her on Wisconsin Avenue in Georgetown and drive back to the country to my husband.

🙙

Donovan tries to convince me there's nothing more I can do; he hates to see the pain of my disappointment. I really don't know what is true or what is possible. I can see that Pam is struggling. I don't believe she has completely given over to the drugs—yet. Of course, there is the allure of the drugs and the drama of street life. But she also wants to reconnect with me, her family, and her church, and to have a real life beyond the shadow of the drugs.

About this time, I read an interview with the head of the National Institute on Drug Abuse (NIDA), who says, "No one wants to be a drug addict. It is a miserable life." I appreciate this woman's compassion, and share her conviction that the drug life is never happy and never really a choice. Most addicts would want to get out if they believed they could, and if they had loved ones who also believed in them.

Whenever Pam calls, she says she wants to get off the drugs, and occasionally tells me how much she misses the church. I assume she is telling me what she thinks I want to hear, but I know a part of her also really does want the freedom of a life without drugs. The NIDA lady's words reverberate: *No one wants to be an addict.*

I want to give Pam the benefit of the doubt.

Also, I'm still surfing the surges of spiritual power that carried me to the heights in Rio Branco. I'm convinced that my determination to save Pam will allow me to harness the power of those waves of spiritual truth which have washed over me. I do not yet realize that the energy of impersonal truth cannot be grasped to serve a personal agenda.

I pray a lot; I ask for a sign. In a *Daime* work I have a vision of Master Irineu in Dupont Circle, reaching his arms out to drug addicts, the way he actually did during his lifetime to alcoholics in Rio Branco, many of whom turned their lives completely around with his help. I dwell in the belief that I am meant to be his arms in Washington D.C., letting the flowers of light brought by the *Daime* vine grow and blossom in the dark places in this city.

I develop a plan. I believe that Pam needs both the *Daime* and conventional drug treatment. Standard treatment models understand the nature of addiction as a disease, and its psychological underpinnings, in a way the church does not. On the other hand, treatment centers often pay only lip service to the reality of the higher power that is so tangibly experienced through the *Daime*. I know that only through surrender to the power of the divine can an addict truly heal. For a long time I've visualized a treatment modality that would combine both; thus I believe that it's my mission to develop a prototype by offering this combination to Pam. I feel confident that Pam would go to day treatment during the week and return to drinking *Daime* during the weekend works if, and probably only if, she could live with me. If she agrees, I will find an apartment where we can live together.

This is a radical idea. It means leaving Donovan, hopefully temporarily, as he does not support this move.

🦋

Pam agrees to the plan. I do not know if this is just for temporary respite or because she's truly ready, but I choose to believe her stated desire to get clean. By mid-July, I sign a year's lease on a small apartment near *Daime* friends. I move my Pathwork counseling practice up to the D.C. area. I can just barely afford this new lifestyle; Donovan reluctantly agrees to anchor our life back at Sevenoaks.

Pamela leaves her dealers and moves in with me. In the space of a week, with donations from friends and trips to Goodwill, we furnish the apartment. We're both especially delighted with the thrift shop purchase of a small but ornately decorated wooden dressing table where Pam and a gay male friend spend hours doing their makeup.

Every weekday I drive Pam to a day treatment facility near us, where she stays all day until I pick her up at 6 p.m. They give her medication to help with the heroin detox, which isn't too bad since this time she's been using for only a few weeks. Together we attend a *Daime* prayer service on Wednesday evenings and another longer ceremony on the weekends.

We make dinner in our tiny kitchen for a couple of young people from the church and she seems to have a good time with them. But she still wants to visit her friends in Dupont Circle.

It's pouring rain one evening when she bugs me to drive her to the nearby subway stop so she can go into the city. I vacillate and obsess about my decision, but eventually agree. I drop Pam off with only enough money for the subway ride.

As I leave the parking area, the inner critic begins: *You shouldn't have trusted her, you should have said no.* These self-critical thoughts blur my mind's clarity just as the sheets of rain blur my eyesight. Pulling out into the street, I fail to notice a car barreling down the main road; it plows into my barely moving car. My head is whipped back onto the seat's headrest. I am otherwise undamaged, and no one in the other car is hurt. Shaking and in shock, I stand out in the rain for an hour waiting for a cop to assess what's obvious: the accident is my fault. I drive home in tears.

When Pam returns, she is very sympathetic to my distress. She convinces me that she has not used drugs, but instead was able to talk to several addict friends about her own recovery and about her work in the church. She joins me in the fantasy of bringing some of these young people into the *Daime* for their own healing.

🙊

One morning three weeks after we start living together, I notice that Pam is spending longer than usual at her dressing table. I compliment her on her taking such good care of her appearance. I drive her to the treatment center and drop her off at the door. It is August 3, 2000.

That afternoon I drive to the treatment center to pick her up. When she's not outside, I go into the office and ask where she is. I'm told that she never came in to treatment that day. My heart sinks into my stomach. When I go to my bank, I discover that someone has tried to use my ATM card, though fortunately Pam did not know my PIN number. Waves of anger inflame my chest. When I return to the apartment, I find a note to me left on her bed:

> *To Mom:*
>
> *Well, I guess this is it, huh? I couldn't handle the truth so lies came so naturally. Don't ever trust me. ☹ So sad but so true... that you can believe. You love me so much that it hurts so bad... don't trust me, please understand. Anyways, what to do next? Liars Anonymous doesn't exist. Lock me away, crazy is she, an angel of evil with good etched deep inside, which no one can find. Breaking the rules comes so easily too, but can't stop feeling the guilt... so where to? Back to the streets? They all love me there, or some they do say, but finding a bed, a warm place to stay? To call my own, the place I call home. Sleeping in alleys is my custom there. So love me or not, to help me is rough. So see where I'm coming from, say what you want, it's gonna be tough. Following guidelines or rules as they say, ain't my cup of tea. God help me live this life of... whatever... I can't even say.*
>
> *Much love, Pammy*

Reading this, I know she's using drugs again. I recognize the sing-song writing style from having read something else she'd written while high on crystal meth. A neighbor tells me he saw a man climb into her window the night before. So, now I know. She's gotten high on meth and gone back to the streets with Billy Bob.

The fragile fantasy of help I've tenderly held out to Pam has been smashed out of my hopeful hands. Lying on the cold tile floor of reality are a hundred soul-shearing shards: all my broken dreams for my daughter.

CHAPTER 18

Complete Defeat

Virginia, August – November 2000

I CALL Donovan, sobbing. He doesn't chastise me or say "I told you so." Instead, he drives over in a friend's pickup truck to help me distribute the furniture I've bought and pack up what we can use back home. I'm so grateful for his kindness.

After posting notices and sorting through the responses, I find a sublet and get out of the year's lease on the apartment. I take some pleasure in smashing Pam's dressing table onto the pavement before throwing the pieces of it into a dumpster. My heart feels almost mortally pierced by the poison arrows of Pam's betrayal and my defeat. I am angry and bitter; I feel ashamed of my trusting and generous nature. I'm haunted by the harsh words the Chapel School counselors had used to advise parents on how to deal with their delinquent children: "If they fool you once, shame on them. If they fool you twice, shame on you." Pam has fooled me many more times than twice.

But was she also fooling herself? Did that good part "etched deep inside" want to believe she was ready for help? Or was she manipulating me so she could have a brief respite before her intended return to the streets?

The emotions of shame, bitterness, anger, and despair tumble around in my psyche like clothes randomly falling into each other in a commercial clothes dryer. Sometimes I am detached, witnessing this emotional upheaval through the glass door of the dryer. At other times my head is caught inside, being flung from one terrible feeling to the next. Shaken and overwhelmed, I am unable to pull the plug on this dizzying turmoil.

For the first time in my life I understand the feeling of revenge: wanting to hurt the person who has hurt me, wanting to *do something* so the intolerable feeling of having been a sucker, a victim, will go away, and I can feel "on top" again. Even though I know that wanting revenge is as bad for my soul as chain-smoking cigarettes would be for my lungs, the only way I can think of restoring my personal dignity is to vow never again to help her. I hate her for the way I feel.

By holding on to the anger I'm avoiding feeling my complete helplessness, the free-fall sensation of the bottom dropping out of my life. Acknowledging defeat in the one thing that matters most to me in life—helping my daughter—is more than I can bear. I find myself taking bizarre actions to maintain the illusion of control. Back home at Sevenoaks, I volunteer to be in charge of a large new building we are constructing as part of our retreat center. I know very little about construction, but figure I can throw myself into the job and learn. Unconsciously I'm trying to replace my failed project of saving Pam with another heroic action. Fortunately, a man who actually has the skills to do the job also volunteers, and I quickly realize the folly of my offer.

I retreat to my house and my life with Donovan. We have a friend living in our house at the time, who's recovering from her own setbacks and disappointments. Every morning Mary Janet and I go to the woods in back of the house and sit in silence at the base of a giant white pine. Then we say a rosary. I use the blue beads that Pamela had been given by the Catholic priest at the Chapel School which he'd brought back from Medjugorje. I'm hoping for a miraculous intervention by the Divine Mother. We follow the prayers of the rosary with a pipe ceremony from the Native American Lakota tradition in which Mary Janet has been trained. I offer heartfelt prayers for Pam, turning her over to a higher power.

Every afternoon Mary Janet and I walk to the river that borders the Sevenoaks property. We practice observing breath and footfall, the passing oaks and pines, the occasional rabbit or fox or heron. We sing to the river. Often at night, Donovan, Mary Janet, and I say prayers and sing hymns at our home altar.

These daily spiritual practices keep me sane. Little by little, my mind lets go of shame and bitterness, releasing the idea that revenge would bring any kind of satisfaction. I accept what is happening: *It is as it is.* I repeat this truth like a mantra.

Finally I am able to let myself be sucked under by waves of helplessness, accepting the watery pummeling and resting afterward on the quiet sand of deep humility. In the midst of this quiet some peace arrives. I can see more clearly that the defeat of the ego does not constitute a fatal wound to my soul. Only my ideas about myself as a hero and my agenda for Pam's life are dying. But they are just ideas, after all, not reality.

What will happen now is anybody's guess.

᎒

With the oily fuel of her own shame and guilt now added to the fire of her addiction, Pam's life rages out of control. She writes:

> Being addicted to heroin is the worst thing ever. Try to imagine something your body needs before you can drink, before you can eat, and before you can sleep. Those are the three basic things God gave to sustain us. When you become addicted, really addicted to heroin, you have to have it in your system in order to be able to receive these three things. That is some

powerful stuff.

My main stretch of serious heroin addiction took place on Georgia Avenue in Washington, D.C. I had been living in Dupont Circle and traveling on the subway to get my heroin on the Avenue. The guy who took me there warned me, "Never come down here alone, or at night." So what do I do? Move there.

The smell is the first thing that stands out in my memory. A mixture of rotten food and fast food wrappers, the heat from the pavement multiplying the acidic aroma. Then a wave of fried food coming from the multiple takeouts where you can order food from people protected behind bulletproof glass. The corner stores sell Newports, two for fifty cents.

There are only two groups of people on this street—the dealers and the users.

Let's start with the dealers. The dealers have an amazing system set up. Better than anywhere else I have been. So obvious, yet somehow they seem to get away with it. They start at seven a.m. They have their parts of the area separated out so each one has his own spot and each has heroin that they give some special name. They come out in shifts. Three guys are out, and they holler the name of the dope they have. You get to know the different types, which one's the best, which one's no good, etc. You can go to one side of the building and if they feel like selling to you, you go through the door. Inside is another man who has the dope. You get your bag—$10 a bag, or $8 if you buy more than five bags. Then you go out the other side. You never really know: Are they going to sell to you or not? Because sometimes they want you to buy from the guys who have the lower-quality stuff. They have their own little system. Now, they don't sell at night, so you have to make sure you get what you need from 8 p.m. until 7 a.m. or else you're gonna get sick, and waiting sick for the dope guy is horrible. They can be mean when they see that you're sick and mess with you.

At night the cocaine guys come out. They have a different system. They don't yell; you gotta know where to go. They sell cocaine to cook into crack or to inject. The dealers live with their families within two or three blocks from where they sell. They don't live with the users—hardly ever—although occasionally a family member will become an addict. Then they usually support the habit but monitor it closely.

The dealers don't use. They smoke a lot of pot, but only when they aren't working. They need to be alert for the jump-outs. Jump-outs are when undercover cops drive by like a normal person, then pull up, jump out, and grab dealers. They do this a lot, but rarely get much. After a jump-out, the dealers go in for a while, which is not good for the addicts. Rarely is someone holding drugs out in the open. They're stashed somewhere. If we hide in the windows and watch, sometimes we can see where and then grab their stash if they turn away for a minute.

I am amazed at the organization these dealers have. It is very different from how we addicts live, although we are organized around making sure we don't get sick. Ever. We sleep where we can, but I consider myself fortunate to have a place on the couch in an abandoned building. I always manage to work my way into the places to be if you're gonna be an addict. Georgia Avenue is no different.

I befriend Teresa, a thirty-year-old mother of four, including a three-year-old who stays with us. Teresa is also a hardcore life-long heroin addict. We stay in a building that has long been con-demned. The door is guarded by Teresa's oldest boy, who also sells heroin. But Teresa being his mother doesn't help us any; we still have to pay for all our dope. We stay in an apartment on the second floor that has a couch and a bed in the bedroom. The fridge is full of rotted food because there's no electricity. Every now and then we get free food and put it in there and eat it until it's too rotten. I cover myself in old moldy clothes to keep warm when I sleep. The guys come up sometimes and bother me for sex, but not often.

There are broken needles everywhere. Many people come from the well-off parts of town to buy dope and shoot up in the other empty apartments. They leave a little heroin in the bags they do, and give them to me when they leave. Every now and then I get dope by helping some new person get dope or shoot up. It is so cold, and I rarely have clean clothes. I have infections.

But all in all I am still in pretty good shape. There are many people who have been using most of their lives and are terribly beat-up. They help me out, and in turn I help them out. I am able to help because I can get money. I am pretty; guys want me. But it's hard. I have to walk a long way to the Spanish part of town to make $20 a guy. Then I walk back and get my heroin. I have to make sure I have enough for the night and what we call a "wake-up." Because no matter how much heroin you do at night, you still have to have some when you wake up.

Pam doesn't call me, and I'm relieved. I have nothing to say to her now. At the same time, I can't stop thinking about her. So I redirect my energy by getting serious about my personal work in Al-Anon, spending some time every day reading the literature and attending two or three meetings a week. I get a sponsor, a woman who is a devotee of an enlightened Indian master, and in addition to her helping me do the work of the Twelve Steps, we have wonderful talks about awakening. We remind each other of the deep truth which we have both touched—that no matter what life looks like on the outside, underneath all is well, all is God, all is One.

Donovan and I hire the services of an intervention specialist, someone who works with families to help get their loved ones into treatment. Steve's style with me is confrontational; he calls me a "turbo-co," meaning he sees my behavior with Pam as exceedingly codependent. He lectures me about how families can "love their addicts to death—literally" by cushioning them from the consequences of their addiction or by enabling their use of drugs.

Steve drills me with his negative axioms about addicts, including, "How do you know an addict is lying?" Answer: "Because his lips are moving." My self-confidence is sufficiently smashed that I assume Steve's right, and I'm wrong to have ever trusted Pam's stated desire to get clean. "But how will we know when she's ready?" I plead. His answer is to leave that decision to him—the expert—and for now just to focus on my own work in Al-Anon. I comply.

When Pam finally calls to tell me she's alive, I only say what Steve has instructed me to say: "When you're ready for treatment, I'll give you the name of someone to call. Until then I don't want to hear what's happening in your life, only that you're still alive." What Steve actually wants me to say is that I won't talk to her again until she's ready for treatment, but I simply can't do that. It would only further break my already wounded heart. I always accept Pam's collect phone calls. And I always add "I love you" at the end of our brief conversations, also contrary to Steve's instructions.

But I do curb my curiosity about her life, and basically stick to Steve's prescribed words. Pam calls me only every three or four weeks to tell me she's still alive; she calls no one else from the church.

I later find out that during this period she ends up in the emergency rooms of several different hospitals with various infections, seeking pain medication when she can't get heroin. She spends a few days at D.C. General Hospital, where she's given some kind of anesthesia that causes her to sleep for two days and wake up having bypassed the worst of heroin detox sickness. After a week in their detox program, she leaves and returns to Georgia Avenue.

Steve suggests I take one book with me called *The Language of*

Letting Go, a daily reader for helping codependents. Under Steve's direction, we make arrangements with the church people: If Pam calls for help of any kind, they are not to respond but instead direct her to talk with Steve. He has told us that he doesn't think much of most treatment programs, but knows a few he respects. He tells us about a treatment center located far away in Mississippi that is effective with young people.

Once again we ask, "How will you know she's ready?" Again, he instructs us, "Trust me, I'll know."

CHAPTER 19

Letting Go of Experts

Rio Branco, Brazil; Mississippi and Virginia, December 2000

AFTER teaching for a week in São Paulo, Donovan and I fly to
Rio Branco, far away from our life in Virginia and our concerns
about Pam. We've been partners in spiritual exploration ever since we
met, and we want to sample together the many different Amazonian
churches that use *ayahuasca* as a religious sacrament.

We participate in ceremonies of the *União do Vegetal*, the *Barquinha*, and several different *Daime* churches. On the night of December
7-8 (midsummer in the Amazon) we will attend our final *Daime* ceremony of this trip. This work honors the Virgin of Conception by singing and dancing all the hymns of Master Irineu all night long. This is
perhaps the single most important work in the *Daime* church calen-
dar, as it celebrates Master Irineu's first vision of the Virgin Mary in
the moon.

A few days before this work is to be held, Donovan decides to join
Pad. Alfredo on a trip deep into the jungle; he sleeps on a riverboat
which is three-deep in hammocks. He participates in this work in a
newly constructed *Daime* church in Ipixuna, a tiny outpost on the
Juruá river, singing and dancing all night in unrelentingly hot and
humid air, while dressed in a long-sleeved shirt and white suit.

I choose to stay in Rio Branco because I feel drawn to attend this
service at Master Irineu's original church, *Alto Santo*, which sits across
from his tomb. The church is now led by Master Irineu's widow Dona

Peregrina, who normally does not welcome outsiders. She accedes to my request only after I plead, *"O Mestre me mandou."* (The Master sent me.)

During the singing that night in the immaculate white-washed church of the founder of the *Daime* path, I feel connected to all the people who drink this sacrament in many places in the world, who are also doing this ceremony at this same time. I am so grateful to that mysterious design that plucked me out of a normal suburban Maryland upbringing and put me here in this church, in this remote town on the edge of the rainforest singing these hymns, receiving the enormous light and love that they generate. I pray for Pam and recall that it's been exactly five years to the day since she ran away with her drug dealer in Salvador, Bahia on this same Brazilian holiday, and began her descent into serious drug use. As the work ends at sunrise, I feel expanded and mellow, confident that my life and Pam's are in benign hands.

As soon as I return to the *Daime* compound, I am met by a Brazilian friend saying she's received a call from Steve, the addiction interventionist who's been helping us. I try to call immediately. After the usual Brazilian long-distance delays, I eventually do connect with Steve.

He tells me that Pam suffered excruciating pain and was taken to a Washington D.C. hospital emergency room where she was diagnosed with serious pelvic inflammatory disease.

She badly needed medical treatment and finally asked for help from a church friend, who told her, as we had instructed, to call Steve. When she called him, Steve told her she needed to agree to go into drug rehab treatment in Mississippi as a condition of receiving the medical help she needed. Steve tells me she agreed, and has now been treated for her disease.

I ask Steve if he is convinced that her desire for drug treatment is genuine, and he assures me that he is confident that Pam is ready for real change. He arranged one-way airfare and put her on the plane; Pam is arriving at rehab today!

Now I just have to get Donovan out of the jungle so we can start our journey back to the States.

৯

As soon as I return home I call Signal, the treatment center in Mississippi, to ask about their rules for communication with clients. I want to know what to do in case Pam calls. I am given to her case-worker, who cheerily shares that she's talking with Pam at that moment and asks if I'd like to say hello. My mouth goes dry and I can barely utter "No, no, I'm not ready to talk to her. I don't know what your rules are."

But she reassures me: "Oh, there's no problem with your just saying hello," and gives the receiver to Pam.

Pam and I have not had a real conversation since before she left the apartment we shared. It was a terribly traumatic ending. Emotionally, I felt like I'd been beaten bloody and nearly unconscious with a two-by-four. How can this counselor assume that we could "just say hello"? She's acting as though my daughter has just arrived for freshman orientation week at college!

Pam asks how I am, and I ask how she is. We then have a ridiculously shallow conversation for the next few minutes. I can't believe it. What is going on here? Later, I call the counselor back and warn her, "Pam is being totally phony with me right now. I expect she's being phony and lying to you as well. Please don't ever again put me in a situation where I need to talk to her like that!" The counselor's reply— that she will honor my need for more structure—feels condescending.

That night Donovan accepts a collect call from Pam. She's hysterical, saying she's going to leave treatment now, this minute. Donovan puts her on speaker phone so I can listen: "I'm so sorry about leaving the apartment with Mom ... how I did it ... how I hurt her and disappointed you both ... I'm just so sorry." She's sobbing, and she sounds sincere. I can't repress my tendency to apologize.

"I'm sorry too, Pam, sorry to have set up a situation you weren't ready for, where you were bound to fail."

I'm so grateful for some realness between us. The water of love flows again, soaking into my parched heart.

Then, adding what Steve has suggested, I say, "Pam, I have to back out and let others help you now, not me. I just can't do it. It's not mine to do. Please, Pam, stay there. Please try to give the program your best. They know what they're doing."

Still crying, Pam insists, "I can't stay here. It's not the right place for me. Please let me come back. Get me a bus ticket back, please, please, please." Donovan and I both make clear we won't do that.

At this point we realize that we're talking with her for more than the allotted fifteen minutes, but her situation seems so precarious we stay on the line. Donovan adds his encouragement: "Just stay, Pam. Stay in the program there until you're clean and we can all talk together. We'll come out for their family program, and we can be together then." At the end of our conversation she says she'll stay, at least until she can see us.

At Steve's urging I send Pam a fax, telling her I won't talk on the phone with her now because I just can't do it. I suggest she talk with Steve or with her counselors at Signal. I also again make clear that we will not support her leaving treatment.

The next day I talk with the counselor to make sure she knows Pam has told us she's going to leave. In a patronizing tone she assures me that Pam's not talking about leaving anymore and seems to be adjusting to the rules of the place. "All the girls are working on self-responsibility," she announces proudly. I hope she's right, and I start to relax.

Steve reassures me, "Don't worry. They're onto her tricks. They're very professional. Just trust them, and don't try to be her therapist."

❧

Three hours later the counselor calls back to tell me Pam has run away. She's left in the middle of a very cold and snowy December day, with only the clothes on her back and, so far as they know, no money. They have no idea where she is.

Now *I* am hysterical.

I hand the phone to Donovan, who puts the phone on speaker and then asks politely, "Please… can you call the state police or someone there to help us track her down?" The counselor—all business now—replies in a chilly voice that once Pam has left their property, they do not call the police. They will send back her few belongings and adjust our bill.

"Are you telling me that you won't even call the state police?" he demands.

"Yes I am. That is our policy and I surely can't break it."

"Will you at least give me their phone number?"

"Oh, of course."

"And you're telling me there's nothing more you can do for us?"

"Well, there's one thing I can do" she answers cheerily. "I'll write you a referral."

We're both stunned. That's *it*? Donovan hangs up and dials the number she's given him. A young man answers and quickly makes it clear that this is not the state police and he is irritated at being disturbed. Signal has given us the wrong number.

Donovan tracks down the right number, and a woman dispatcher with a sympathetic voice answers. He describes the situation: our drug-addicted daughter has run away from treatment and is on the highway in the snow in Mississippi, with no money and no coat.

The woman asks Donovan where he's calling from and sounds

surprised at his answer. "You're all the way up in Virginia? Signal's right close to us here—why aren't they calling?"

"Ma'am, I wish I knew the answer to that."

When we hang up, Donovan is fuming at the way Signal has treated us, and at their worthless offer to write a referral.

Naturally, my own first impulse is to blame myself. My self-flagellation kit now includes even more whips and chains, fashioned from Steve's accusation that I'm "turbo-codependent." My thinking goes something like this: *Is contact with me so toxic that just knowing I'm still here, still loving her, feeds a belief that I will magically save her? That she doesn't have to make the effort to save herself? Must I completely cut her off, as Steve has been urging? Will she only find in herself the motivation to change if I'm completely out of the picture?*

I'm all twisted up inside. *Is my love for my daughter killing her?*

❧

That night standing in front of my bathroom sink, I look in the mirror and see an unfamiliar reflection—it's the saddest face I've ever seen. It looks like the face of Mary in Italian Pietà paintings grieving her dead son. Looking at that face, I want to cry.

My mind goes blank. I'm no longer blaming anyone or anything. Pam has run away again. It happened, it just happened. But then the sadness starts to well up from deep inside. First my gut clenches, then my heart breaks, and then I begin to wail. I hang on to the side of the sink; the grief is so intense I can barely stand up. I have never felt emotional pain like this.

And then it gets worse. I slump to the floor, unable to stand.

I find myself wondering how a human body can handle so much pain. I have a fleeting vision of the body starting to break apart—limbs hurtling through space. An arm breaking into pieces as it smashes on the brown tile floor, a foot flying into the toilet, the head bursting into a million shreds of white bone and grey matter. The picture of my exploding brain suddenly seems very funny and I burst out laughing, completely baffling Donovan, who sits helpless and sad by my side.

Finally the grief subsides and I feel washed clean. I realize that I haven't had any negative thoughts about myself or Pam during this entire earthquake of grief. I'm not thinking that this latest crisis shouldn't have happened. I'm not thinking she's wrong or I'm wrong. It's just plain painful—my beloved daughter out alone in the middle of winter in rural Mississippi, out of her mind, still addicted to the worst possible drugs, and now vulnerable to whatever random killers or rapists she might run into.

The next night is Saturday and there are no Al-Anon meetings, so I make it to an open AA meeting and tearfully tell my story. The wife of a longtime AA member is there, having herself spent many years in the Al-Anon program. She talks to me for an hour after the meeting, and together we go over and over the first three steps: 1) accept my powerlessness; 2) believe in a power greater than myself; and 3) turn my life and will over to that higher power. I turn Pam over to her higher power at least five hundred times during the next few days, praying for her constantly and praying that I may continue to receive the grace to let her go.

🙆

Pam writes:

I call my mom and beg her to bring me back to D.C. She says, "If you want to come back, you'll have to make it back on your own. I will not support your decision to leave treatment." That makes my blood boil. How can she think that would stop me? I leave that day, walking out in the snow in the backwoods of Mississippi.

I reach the nearest town and, with the $50 that a roommate has given me, I immediately buy a pack of needles at the drug store. I don't know when or where I'll find something to shoot up, but when I do, I want to be ready.

I wander around the small town and, sure enough, find drugs. I find a guy who smokes crack, and he convinces me to spend the rest of my money buying crack. Now, I know you can shoot up crack if you break it down with lemon juice. I'm still at a time in my addiction when I'm obsessed with shooting up. I don't want to smoke anything; I want it in my arm. But we have no lemon juice, so I decide to try it with alcohol—rum, to be exact.

We're in an abandoned building. I take some of the crack and a spoon, and while he sits there and smokes up the crack, I try to break it down with rum. It doesn't work. I shoot up rum. I don't get high at all and I'm so mad. And he has smoked up what I don't have in the spoon. So that really pisses me off.

I hitchhike in semis all the way back to D.C. without getting raped or killed. I guess my angels are watching over me. I know everything happens for a reason.

❧

Steve, who had assured us a few weeks ago that he was confident Pam was ready for treatment, calls to say he's convinced Pam left because the professionals at the treatment center were on to her games.

Something snaps. I've had it with experts. *Really* had it. I'm sick of the superiority of people who think they know my addicted daughter better than I do. I'm fed up with believing people who make me feel bad for loving her.

At the same time, I know it's time to let go of the rope that has kept me attached to my daughter and trying so hard to help her. My hands and heart are raw from rope burn.

Five days after running away from Signal Treatment Center, Pam calls. It's Christmas Eve and she's just returned to D.C. I'm relieved she's alive. Neither Pam nor I suggest further contact.

I realize something in me has let go—the rope is out of my hands. She's on her own. She has miraculously made it back to D.C. unscathed. Whatever is in charge of her life will do with her whatever it does. She'll survive or she won't. It's not up to me.

That night I go to the traditional Christmas Eve *Daime* ceremony. While this is normally a celebratory work, tonight is our farewell to Helena, the founder of this church, who is now in the final stages of her terminal cancer. She will die a month later. The sadness of the evening feels familiar and oddly comforting to me.

CHAPTER 20

Wild Child

California, January – October 2001

THREE weeks later Pam calls to tell me she's going to California with a friend whose parents have given them both one-way bus tickets to San Diego.

In my next *Daime* work, after my daughter is already on the Greyhound bus, I hear Pam's voice clearly speaking these words, "I must be about my Father's business." Now, this is what Jesus supposedly said when he began his ministry. It's a bizarre parallel. My daughter's off to be a full-time drug addict in every addict's idea of paradise—southern California, where sunshine and drugs are plentiful—and she's telling me the same thing that the major spiritual avatar of the West told his family when he left home to launch his teaching mission. All I can do is smile in puzzlement. I accept that Pam is impelled by something larger than herself to make this pilgrimage. Still, this is not exactly my idea of a spiritual journey.

🔊

Pam writes:

When I get on the Greyhound with Susie, we have three duffel bags full of stolen stuff. We also have our permanent goods, which consist of a little bag with our needles, Q-tips, lots of empty heroin baggies, and a spoon, broken halfway down the handle.

I down half a bottle of Nyquil—Susie drinks the other half—and as my eyes close, I hope I will wake up in San Diego. We make numerous stops but eventually I do fully wake up in San Diego. Ironically, all our bags of stolen goods have been stolen during the trip.

We make our way to a restaurant where we meet some military guys who pay for our food. Then we get on their bus into the city, intriguing them with tales of our travel and drug use. They get us a hotel room and go off to their army base, and we never see them again. They were just friendly strangers.

When we wake up we take care of our first order of business, finding a fix. It takes about twenty minutes. (Addicts always know just where to find drugs, no matter where they are.) Next Susie begins to show me the ropes of life as a San Diego street kid, which is very different from D.C. She shows me how to hitch free rides on the trolley, all the places to sleep, and where to get food. She introduces me to a dozen other kids.

After about three weeks Pam loses contact with Susie, but in short order hooks up with another addict.

The day I meet Adam, he's sitting on top of a hill in Mario Park in San Diego. He's with his friend Matt. They ask if I want to go get something to eat and of course I do. They are both clean, normal-looking guys. I have no idea they're fellow drug addicts, street kids. We go and get something to eat, then they take me back to where they're staying.

They introduce me to their two other friends, Casey and Genevieve. Casey is mentally ill. I find out later he had been hit by a car when he was eleven years old and gotten a huge amount of money to be dispersed to him monthly after he turned eighteen, which had just happened. So Adam, Matt, and Genevieve had befriended him and were spending his money, with which he was very generous. He's a great find! Adam decides I can get a lot of money from Casey just by flirting with him, so I do. And sure enough, I just ask him for $200 and he gives it to me. I tell Adam I'll be back later and leave. He follows me outside and asks if I do drugs. I tell him yes. Then he tells me he does heroin, so it's fine after that. We get some and get high. It's the beginning of a long descent into codependent insanity.

Adam and I don't separate for a long time after that. We do everything together. It gets to the point where we fight about who will do the last shot of dope if there's only enough for one of us. He insists that I do it, and I say he should do it. We share everything. If someone invites one of us to stay at their house or get a shower and the other isn't invited, we don't go. We'd rather sleep in a park than be separate.

Together we juice Casey for lots and lots of money. When that gets old, we start camping on the Mexico/California border and crossing the bridge every day to buy heroin and coke, which you can get in little stores in Tijuana if you know where to go. Adam has no fear at all; he asks until we find the best ones. Then we go every day. Money from Adam's grandmother, sent frequently, helps support our habit.

Getting back from Mexico is easy—I carry drugs inside my body. You go through a check and just tell them all you're bringing back is a hangover and a stomachache. Adam is great at getting us through with no questions asked. One trip, however, I stupidly have my needle up my coat sleeve and we get pulled to the side. They search us, even the bag of Doritos I'm carrying. They're getting ready to search our clothes and I stick my tummy out as far as it will go and ask if I can please use the bathroom, because I am pregnant. They let us go.

After getting back across we go directly to a McDonald's. I put a cap on to look like a guy and we go into the handicapped bathroom stall. Adam always puts wet toilet paper on the cracks on the door. We shoot up coke and heroin.

One time I can't get in the men's room. Adam goes and does his share, and when he comes out he gives me the bags. I go in thinking he has separated out my part and so what remains is mine to do. I shoot up, and the next thing I remember is waking up with him asking me if I had done all the rest of the coke. I had done about four times more than I should have and it would have killed most people. It's a miracle that I survived. At the time I think it's cool that I'm so messed up.

After running around San Diego for a while we get a bus to Los Angeles. L.A. is a place I will never return to. Ever.

We always find the people we need to know in the lifestyle within hours of being in a new place. You can smell them. We stay in an abandoned building with a few other people. We hook up with a guy who has meth and start hanging with him. This guy called Dude is very disturbed. He gets his money and drugs by being a play toy for an older gay man. A few weeks into L.A., Adam, Dude, and I take a bus to another part of town. Dude asks Adam to go with him and says they'll meet me back at the house. This is the first time Adam has agreed to separate from me. I have a fit. I don't know how to get back to the building where we're staying. They walk off, and I realize two seconds later that they forgot to give me any bus tokens. I try to catch up, but somehow they've disappeared. I don't see Adam again for a week.

I call my parents, completely a mess, and beg for help. I can't stand losing Adam.

In April Donovan and I are going to lead a workshop in Southern California, so when Pam calls, he decides to go early and see if he can get her into rehab. This time *I'm* the skeptical one. I feel pretty sure Pam is just missing her boyfriend, not really ready to end the drug life.

❧

I try to practice detachment. I make a sad joke about Pam, saying I can be certain of only one thing now that she's in southern California: at least she won't freeze to death.

Pam's marginal life underscores the universal truth that life in a physical body always hangs by a thread. Parents of teenagers have always had to face the precarious nature of their child's physical existence, whether they are handing the keys to the family car to their son or daughter, or kissing their young soldier goodbye. When I look at my life circumstances from this larger perspective, I realize I have an opportunity to practice equanimity in the face of the universal uncertainties of life. This brings me some freedom.

When a friend tells me about her college-age daughter who will be studying at the Sorbonne in Paris next year, I make up a story for myself about how my daughter is choosing to explore the parks and streets of southern California this year. At first I think that's a pretty pathetic way to amuse myself, but then I realize I really *don't* know. Maybe Pam's explorations of street life will prove as important to her future as my friend's daughter's year at the Sorbonne will be for her.

❧

Pam writes:

My dad decides to fly out if I'll agree to go to rehab. The day I'm supposed to meet him I'm on a bus and I see Adam walking down the street. I jump out and grab him. Something's wrong. He shows me papers saying he was arrested on assault charges. Dude had tricked him and taken him to a hotel room with two gay men who overamped him on meth. This is the term they use because it's difficult to OD on meth and die, but you can overamp, which means you feel like you might die but you don't. Adam pulls up his shirt to show me the circles on his chest where he'd had heart monitors attached to him at the hospital. He tells me that when the men tried to rape him he stabbed one of them, cutting him very badly. That's why they had shot him up with that much meth.

I will never know what really happened to Adam that week. The alternate reality one lives in while on meth is usually very far from what is actually happening. But the police papers and the circles on his chest indicate it was serious.

My dad stays in a motel but Adam and I are too high to be in there. We don't sleep that night, as is the case most nights. We hover in corners and shadows until morning comes.

The next day the three of us begin the drive to San Diego where there's a treatment center that will take me. Adam urges me to go. When we get to San Diego we sit down to eat in a restaurant. I tell my dad to wait there for a minute while Adam and I get a newspaper. We leave, and never return.

That's the beginning of the end of Adam and me.

Adam is really affected by the meth. Everyone is, but it's evident to me that he has really gone into an alternate reality that he believes is real. Most of the time when I'm on meth, I know very well that I'm high and my crazy experiences are a drug-induced insanity. I just think it's fun to live in a fake reality. But Adam doesn't know the difference, and it gets bad very quickly. I think his experience in L.A. had a terrible effect on him. He's so sure there are people after us all the time. He disappears for hours at a stretch, and we fight a lot. Once, when I threaten to leave him, he even stabs himself in the leg. As our insanity gets worse our relationship fades, and I decide to leave him.

Sitting on top of a newspaper stand in front of the Greyhound bus terminal in San Diego, I watch him disappear into the station. I will never see him again.

Apparently, while in the station Adam goes nuts, believing a man coming out of the restroom is going to rape me (even though I'm not there), and he attacks the man violently. Adam was conceived when his mother was raped, and I believe he was—in his own crazy way—trying to defend her and me by attacking this stranger. Naturally, he ends up in jail, where he also attacks some guards, so he has been permanently branded a violent psychotic drug addict, and now a convicted felon.

I expect he has not pulled out of his insanity and is rotting away in prison in California, probably still living in an alternate universe, one into which he was thrown permanently by crystal meth. I will always feel guilty for introducing Adam to meth.

୬

It doesn't surprise me when Pamela runs away from Donovan in San Diego before they get to the treatment center. At least he has gotten her out of the more dangerous drug scene in L.A. When I meet Donovan at the airport in California, he looks drained. I know the feeling.

After the workshop, on Easter morning, Donovan and I do a ceremony with a *Daime* church group high up in a California canyon. We watch the rising sun creep up the canyon walls. We read the Easter story.

I am taken back to an Easter service I witnessed as a child while attending my friend's Episcopal church. On Good Friday a large black cross all but obliterated the altar at the front of the church. Then on Easter morning everyone brought flowers and one by one pinned those flowers all over the cross until it fairly glowed with springtime. As a child, I was filled with the sense that I was being initiated into a great mystery about life and death, one that went way beyond the rational linear world view of my agnostic parents who believed that life ended with the death of the body.

Now I remember scenes from my time in Master Irineu's tomb, along with the realization that it was in this place of death that I'd felt most deeply alive.

As we continue to sit in silence with eyes closed, a vivid image appears—a woman is coming toward me dressed in Biblical clothing. It is Mary Magdalene. She takes my hand and leads me into the rock tomb where the body of Jesus is supposed to be laid. It's not there, but we both see a brilliant angel of light keeping watch. As we approach him we recognize that he is Jesus himself. I stand before the figure of Jesus and have only one thing to say to him: "Please protect my daughter." He replies, "Trust my care of her."

I visualize Jesus weaving a safety net beneath the razor-sharp tightrope my daughter is walking.

🐾

The next call we get is from the San Diego jail where Pam spends her twentieth birthday serving a sentence for loitering. Enforced detox in jail clears her mind enough to want to get clean, and she agrees to go to the treatment center in San Diego. Friends of ours who live in the area kindly pick her up and take her there. Less than two weeks into treatment, she runs away. Soon Pam takes up residence in the woods in San Diego, home to the delinquent and the discarded.

There is a riverbed in San Diego crossed by three bridges: the trolley, the train, and the freeway. Under these three bridges exists a world that is unknown to most people. It is home to a mix of old and young—the homeless, the outcast, and those who have forgotten the outside world. Almost everyone who lives there has been on crystal meth so long that they live in their own reality. There are camps of people in some places, and elsewhere there are makeshift tents falling apart and belongings scattered, half covered in brush and dirt, holding only the memory of what was someone's home. The river flows in some places, and this is where we clean the scum off our bodies after days awake and trekking through the woods looking for something that can never be found.

I see a bike leaning against a tree behind what looks like a big bush. I go to look, and on the other side of the big bush is an opening in the ground. I see an old man there who tells me that the government has a secret buried underground where the bridges create an X above ground. It's a big conspiracy that I could never understand. He has dug a huge hole in the ground underneath the trees and bushes, and he lives there in his own little world. The cops come sometimes and try to convince him to move to a free room in a nursing home they've arranged for him, but he won't go. This is his home.

Every now and then a stranger comes, going from camp to camp with a little notebook mapping out the path through the woods. We always know that the police will follow shortly, following the map so they can find the people sheltered there.

I get my drugs by flirting with guys. They give me meth and I say I have to use the bathroom and disappear into the woods, thinking I can hear them chasing me. They never are. I create hiding places. I spend hours in the bushes and bamboo making forts for myself, hearing noises and seeing shadow people.

Once, after a shot of crystal, I walk along a path at the top of the riverbed. I see what looks like another path and go down it. I get lost and spend all night trying to find my way. I light my lighter at one point and see a huge spider. I believe I have spiders all in my hair and clothes. I panic and strip naked. I lose my shirt and shoes so I rip a piece of my pants and tie it around my top. I finally climb up a steep incline early in the morning and end up at the highway with branches sticking in my hair. I wonder what the morning commuters must think.

Once I am with a bunch of people who give me money to go buy sodas. When I return and hand them their sodas, they ask where I've been. Apparently I've been gone for two whole days; I have no idea where I've been. Others living in the woods have similar experiences. We are each in a reality created solely by our own minds. It's fun, in a totally weird way.

Some of us come out of the woods into the parking lot of the football stadium after the games start, and we find lots of food left behind from people's tailgate parties. That food is so yummy. We set the car alarms off, then break windows and steal things out of the cars. It's like paradise for us. We get food and stuff we can trade for drugs. One of the things about California is that you can trade things for drugs, which makes it easier. Living in the woods and stealing go well together because hardly anyone will dare run into those woods after you if they happen to see you stealing.

We go up into the housing developments at night and go through garbage. We can run all night doing this. One night I pull a big box of clothes out of a dumpster and I'm sitting on the curb looking at it when I realize there are ants all over me. They are on their way to the dumpster and I have interrupted them. They are not happy with me; it's gross. Being high on meth makes it all much worse. I have scabies, and that make me feel like I have stuff crawling on me all the time. I can see them under my skin and try to pick them out with tweezers and needles, but I never get anything.

We run the streets all night and retreat to the woods in the day, unless we're lucky enough to find someone to let us in their home or get us a hotel room. But usually only one or two people get lucky at a time.

🙠

Pam steals money from a guy who had promised her drugs. When he finds her on the beach, he dumps beer on her, flashes a gun, and says he's going to mess her up bad. Two women nearby—green-haired Mohawk-coifed lesbians—come to her rescue. They grab some brooms leaning against the wall of a nearby taco shop and, like good witches, fight him off with their broomsticks.

Pam is convinced this man means to kill her, and she also knows she has nowhere to hide in San Diego. Even if he doesn't kill her, someone else here might. It's payback time, which means it's time to leave town. Pam goes with the lesbians to hitchhike up to San Francisco to go to a Halloween party they've heard about.

If I stayed in San Diego I'd be dead. So I'm going to San Francisco. But I'll just do the same stuff there. So I'll probably die there... or maybe not... who knows? Maybe a miracle will happen.

Even though the drugs are running my life now, the truth the *Daime* showed me is always with me. I never forget that God is real and that whatever happens is part of God's plan for my life. I'm not afraid of death. If I die, I die. A part of me is just watching this crazy drama that is my life. I know there is something deeper than this, something that isn't affected by my drama, something that won't die. I also know God could do for me what I cannot now do for myself. I wonder what will happen.

CHAPTER 21

Hitting Bottom

Virginia, January – October 2001

P AM's in California learning what it takes to survive as a drug-addicted street person. Now it's my turn to learn the survival skills of a codependent.

First I need to take another good hard look at my remaining addiction to saving my daughter. Pam is three thousand miles away in a city where I could never find her, much less rescue her from herself. Under these circumstances any belief that her recovery is up to me is, clearly, a form of madness.

I watched the grandmother of Adam—Pam's California boyfriend—live out this kind of insanity. Whenever Adam said he needed money for food, Grandma Emma sent it to him (even though I told her that Pam said he was just using the money for drugs). She believed every paranoid tale and every manipulative lie Adam told her. In her mind she was convinced she could save her grandson through her devotion and prayer. In reality Adam was just going from bad to worse and Grandma Emma was going broke.

Pam knows that I will not send her any money or bail her out of any jams; she no longer asks us for anything. If this is the life she wants, she will have to experience the full brunt of its consequences, until the pain of using becomes worse than the pain of stopping. Or until she dies.

But, while I can cease any actions that might enable Pam's drug

use, I cannot control the thoughts in my mind. What I can do is ob-
serve them carefully. I discover that I really think only a few things, but
I think them constantly. It's the Pam Channel, round the clock: *Where
is she? Will she ever make it back? What should I do? What should I say
when she calls next?* These same thoughts pop up as often as spam pops
up on my computer, but there's no easy way to delete them

As I practice observing my mind, I can sometimes bring attention to the background space behind all this rat-a-tat rapid firing of the
worry neurons. If attention is held in the silence between thoughts,
a deeper level of awareness sometimes arrives. This larger space is
utterly relaxed and easy. When consciousness rests in that empty
space, there is respite.

More often, however, my attention is caught by the bright neon
fears about all the terrible things that might happen to Pam. At those
moments all I can do is watch the alarm that grabs my gut, pours
adrenalin into my system and puts my mind in high gear. All I can do is
pray to be spared from the horror of believing my thoughts.

I often repeat an Al-Anon slogan: "Don't just do something, stand
there!" I try to hold my ground against the temptation to believe my
mind's flashing red dashboard demand that *This is an emergency and I
must do something* to save Pam. I do a few practical things for myself,
like posting a list of simple DOs and DON'Ts at the telephone where
I receive Pam's calls.

DON'T	DO
Panic	Stay calm, no matter what
Push help at her	Let her know help is available
Tell her what to do	Hear what she is doing for herself
Try to control	Surrender to what is

I also post a *New Yorker* cartoon of a mother rushing into her
skinny son's bedroom where he is diligently lifting weights. The mom

bursts in yelling, "Oh, can I help?" Yep, that's me all right.

I ask myself seriously: what exactly is the unconscious belief that keeps fueling my obsession with Pam? It goes like this: *Something is terribly wrong with Pam and it's up to me to fix it.* This comes down to: *Whether Pam lives or dies is up to me. My constant loving attention is the umbilical cord keeping her alive; if I stop thinking and worrying about her, she will die.* Donovan labels this belief my illusion of self-importance, and calls it my central illusion. By calling it an illusion, I get enough distance to start questioning: *Is Pam's life or death really dependent on me? Is it really up to me to fix her?* My mind knows these beliefs are false, but my heart and gut cannot let go.

Daily I admit my personal powerlessness. I turn my life and hers over to a Higher Power. I affirm that her life and death are in God's hands, not mine. I sit with the reality that I have no idea what is best for her now.

Every day is like stumbling up a mountain covered in fog so dense I cannot see more than a foot ahead. Keeping my balance can be done only one step at a time. It's not even one day at a time, it's second by second. I watch the mind wanting to grab at answers or conclusions, at lessens learned, at future plans, trying to anchor itself with a piton pounded into the sheer rock face of uncertainty. But there are no pitons to grasp, no ropes to hold, no ledges to step on. There is only this breath, this moment.

❧

In June 2001, I am diagnosed with a tumor on my right ovary. I've had an intermittent pain in my lower right abdomen for a long time, going back to before the time when Pam was in the Chapel School and I found relief from my gut-twisting guilt by receiving the forgiveness of Mother Ocean. Recently a pinching abdominal pain has become more frequent and now I've been given a physical explanation.

When I get the diagnosis, I'm immediately reminded of what I've read in Al-Anon literature: family members can also suffer physical effects from the disease of addiction. Living with this disease can be lethal, and not just for the addict. I feel especially spooked when I remember that it was also the right ovary that was removed from Pam at that inadequate Brazilian hospital when she was fourteen years old. Is our deep connection going to turn fatal for both of us?

The only way to know if the tumor is malignant is to operate. The surgeon recommends taking out both ovaries since if one tumor is growing, another might also, and any tumor can turn cancerous even if it is not now. So I set a date for surgery—August 3—which is exactly a year from the day Pam left our apartment, the last day I saw her.

In our next phone call I tell Pam about my upcoming surgery, but she doesn't respond. She's probably so "out there" on drugs that she does not even understand what I am saying. Instead, she tells me terrible details about sleeping in the woods and eating out of dumpsters. Talking to her feels like having hot cooking oil jump out of the telephone onto my skin. After we hang up, I hear in my head the voice of the addiction expert, a voice I've internalized and which I call my Al-anon Nazi. It tells me I should stop all contact with Pam. But, in my heart I know that not talking to her would feel worse—like being thrown into a freezing abyss of perpetual loneliness.

I go into a slump and now my thoughts are even darker: I imagine telling Pam I have terminal cancer, wondering if even that would impact her. I imagine saying goodbye to this life. I feel acutely my love for Donovan and the loss I would feel to have to leave him. Donovan is certain I don't have cancer, but I don't believe him. I'm also aware that there is a part of me that feels like giving up. This life is just too hard; I'm not sure I have it in me to take much more. Is it over?

ℐ

In July, after teaching in Brazil, I go to the Mauá *Daime* community for a personal retreat. I have until August 3 for my own spiritual healing before I go under the knife. My retreat plan is to be alone in a cabin in the mountains, to fast and do a *Daime* work every day for three days.

In the first work I have the intention to confront my own death. I remember that this is how Ramana Maharshi, the great Indian sage, had his early enlightenment; he invited an experience of death. In fact all I experience are conventional pictures and stories my mind makes up about what my death would look like: pictures of a failing body, saying goodbye to my loved ones, feeling sad. I acknowledge that I have no idea what death is.

In the final work, I walk to a rock outcropping where I can sit and view the mountains. At first the mind is again busy, with thoughts of Pam grabbing my attention. Then suddenly the mind lets go and everything is utterly clear. I AM; always have been and always will be. What I AM is only temporarily clothed in this body-mind.

In these few moments of union with Being, I realize that I don't need to worry about dying because the person I thought I was as Susan has already died. That Susan was full of preferences: she wanted Pam to stop using drugs, my body to heal, my life to be long. But at this moment I have no preferences, no attachment to the outcome of the surgery or the outcome of Pam's life on the streets. Whatever will happen will just happen; it's all okay. It doesn't really matter to the living presence that is here/now beneath the story of Susan. What a relief.

I end the retreat singing the final hymns of Master Irineu, dancing outside in the flowing green grace of these beautiful Brazilian mountains.

⨀

On August 3, at the University of Virginia hospital, I wake up in the recovery room feeling like I've landed in Purgatory. I hear groans of pain and muffled voices, and sense an atmosphere of suffering, depression and fear. I do not know the results of the surgery, and do not want to hear from anyone but Donovan. My abdomen is excruciatingly tender. Soon my own moans join the dismal chorus. I hear the word "morphine" and start fading in and out of consciousness. After a long time, I'm taken to a room where Donovan and my women friends are waiting.

He tells me all is well: the tumor was benign. A part of me is so detached that I don't feel that it matters much either way. But of course I am also relieved because I feel I don't have it in me to battle serious illness. Donovan reminds me that he was always certain it was not cancer. Then he adds, "But it's nice to have a second opinion!"

Returning home, I feel intensely vulnerable, like an infant. There's a sensation of free-fall. Barbara holds me and Mary Janet sings me hymns. They bring in pictures of Mother Mary with the infant Jesus. I breathe in the simple, sweet confidence and trust between Mother and child. I breathe out the fear of coming fully into this body.

I develop a fever and need more antibiotics. I have serious bruising that takes a long time to heal. My recovery is very slow. Sensations are very intense and slowed down; I spend an hour eating a bowl of soup.

I feel a new body growing. I spend hours enjoying the intense experience of just being. Many psychic wires get re-connected: I do not need to save Pamela, or help anybody else or serve the planet, or do anything at all to be worthwhile. I can receive and enjoy each moment just as it is and that is enough. My prayer becomes: "Only You, Mother, there is only you."

❧

In late August Pam calls.

"I'm still alive," she announces.

"I'm glad."

"But the only reason I want to live at all is you."

"Well, Pam, you know I love you and I always will."

"I know. But life sucks."

"I expect it's pretty hard out there. Are you ready to come off the streets and to get clean?"

"I don't know, Mom, I just don't know."

"When you're ready, I'll support you."

"Yeah. Yeah. Gotta go now."

"Okay, stay in touch."

"Okay."

I conclude the call as I always do, "I love you Pam. Goodbye."

Neither of us mentions my surgery.

❧

September 11: I miss Pam all over again. In the face of this col-lective tragedy, when most families are drawing close, her absence is a gaping crater in the ground I stand on. In Al-Anon I share that I expect that we who live or have lived with the disease of alcoholism or drug addiction are perhaps better prepared to tolerate the collec-tive horror that is now among us. We've lived with shock, disappoint-ment and terror.

Donovan and I fly to Brazil shortly after 9/11. The plane is almost empty; I'm amused that people are too frightened to fly. Next to my real life concerns, the prospect of a plane to Brazil being hijacked by terrorists seems pretty remote. When we land in Rio, we see a bill-board-sized photo of the *Cristo Redentor*—the famous statue of Christ with outstretched arms standing on the hill of Corcovado—with this heartfelt condolence: *"O Rio Abraça Nova Yorque"* (Rio Embraces New York). People in the streets come up to us to offer condolences. I gratefully hug many strangers that day on the streets of Rio and cry with them. I do not share my private grief.

Sitting with friends outside a *Daime* church in Rio, I look up at the moon, as I do frequently when my heart is aching from missing Pam. Quietly I hum to myself the simple tune of a children's song that has been stuck in my mind ever since the moon sent me to Omaha to rescue Pam: *"I see the moon, the moon sees me, the moon sees the one that I want to see. … "* Letting myself be penetrated by the moon's soft light, feeling the quiet brilliance of my Divine Mother, I am always comforted.

Tonight the moon is full and she speaks to me, whispering that I will be going soon to California to pick up Pam. The moon assures me, "the call will come." Of course I don't know whether this will be the call from a morgue, or the call from Pam saying she's ready for treatment. At this point, either call would be a relief.

In October I get a call from Pam that she is now in San Francisco. I ask if she is ready to get off the streets and for the first time she says, "Yes."

"Are you ready to go into treatment to get clean?"

She doesn't answer; she's waffling. Donovan warns me not to get my hopes up. I cannot help feeling, however, that this is the first step in the dance of her coming home.

Pam writes:
San Francisco is a city I could go the rest of my life without visiting again. It's almost like the cities get worse as you go up the coast. San Francisco is full of long-time drug users. These people are old pros at manipulating and living homeless. They're so used to it, it's like they've never lived any other way.

There is a big bridge under the freeway where they set up camp. I begin to shoot heroin here. Same drugs, same rules, same misery, just a new place. I panhandle in front of stores for cigarettes and money. I get lucky sometimes and can find a trick to make a chunk of money, but mostly I am just getting by. I'm no longer really getting high, just pacifying the drug demon so I don't get sick. I don't know how to get out. I'm just living from fix to fix; I can't go on much longer. In my heart I'm praying to God to help me find a way out, or a way to die.

Chapter 22

Miracle on the Street

California, November 2001

Pam has not just hit bottom; she's living there. Like a bottom-feeding fish in a deep ocean, she doesn't seem to have any way to swim upward toward the light.

I am living my own bottom, as our lady of perpetual sorrow. I'm functioning, but a large part of me is on hold, just waiting for "the call."

๛

Pam writes:

I walk to the Walgreens up the street from where I'm staying under the freeway bridge in San Francisco. I'm so sick. I'm wearing pink bunny slippers and they're all wet from walking in the puddles and streams under the bridge that are hard to avoid when it rains. And it's still raining. I sit against the wall outside the store. Already at a point where I am not able to move easily, I have stomach cramps and blurred vision. I have to get some money for a fix soon. If I can't I'll have to get to a hospital. I begin asking for change as people come in and out of the store.

A man rides up on his bike and comments that I make a dry patch on the ground. He looks kind of beat-up, like a dude who probably smokes, so I ask him for a cigarette. He smiles, pauses and looks at me, then gives me a cigarette and enters the store. I figure I'll hit him up for money when he comes out. His eyes are bright blue and seem to have light coming from them.

I just want some money, and to not hurt anymore. Getting clean really doesn't seem like an option; the idea is not at all in my head at that moment. The guy comes out of the store and stands next to me. He doesn't sit down; he stands, but I don't feel like he's looking down at me. His eyes are so blue on such a grey day. He sparkles, and I hurt.

He's my angel, but I don't know it yet.

He seems to know my situation and I say yes, I'm a heroin addict. He says, simply, "I will give you some cigarettes and my phone number. If you want some help, a way out, call me this evening and I will see what I can do. I'll talk to my wife and I'll see if we can help."

I'm normally turned off by guys. You never know what they might want and I'm too sick to turn a trick. I don't even beg for money like I usually do. I just say okay. And then he leaves.

I must have gotten a fix somehow because my next memory is being at a payphone far away from Walgreens; I wouldn't have been able to get there without some dope first. Now, it's strange that I'm even thinking about calling because usually, after I get high, I'm not worried about being "helped" in any way other than a place to sleep or more drugs or money. I have a feeling this guy isn't any of those things. I say to myself, "Oh, God, here we go again, another trick."

But then I remember his mentioning he had a wife. And I remember the light in his eyes. That light is somehow familiar, it reminds me of the light I once knew back when I was drinking *Daime*. I figure I might as well give it a shot. What the hell? So I call.

I'm not really sure how I get there, but my next memory is sitting in his apartment, and I feel safe. Finally, I feel safe. The first thing Jeff tells me is that he has methadone, so I won't be sick. He doesn't say "Have sex with me" or "Don't steal my stuff." He doesn't say, "You're a loser, and I'm better because I'm clean." He knows exactly what I need. He gives me methadone. His wife Karen makes me a peanut butter sandwich and lets me take a bath. She shows me how to clean out the abscesses that are developing on my legs. I can hardly believe the total respect they show for me. They completely know where I'm coming from and they say they'll be there for me as long as I need them.

Then Karen gets some pot and we all three smoke together. Jeff grows his own medical marijuana and after we smoke we talk and talk. They tell me about themselves. Jeff and Karen are devoted to each other; they're recovering addicts who have used drugs more years than I have been alive, and have suffered pains that I know nothing about. They were on the streets for years, hauling their belongings around in a grocery cart. They were abandoned by their families long ago. They are both HIV positive, have Hep C, and are already pretty sick. Karen injected herself with HIV when she found out Jeff had it, because she didn't want to be separate from him in any way. Her arms are also covered with scars from having cut herself as a young mental ward patient. She still occasionally cuts herself when the pain gets too bad. But they've gotten their lives together enough to have a subsidized apartment, and disability money to live on.

That night I hear so much about their lives on the street that I learn exactly what's ahead for me if don't get free from the stranglehold of my addiction.

After two days of being with them, I'm ready to call my mom. I tell her I'm really done this time. It's over. This is it. I'm so sick and tired of being sick and tired. All I want is to get and stay clean, and I'll do whatever it takes. I ask if she can come out and bring me back to the East Coast so I can get really clean there.

ॐ

The call comes on November 14. Pam tells me she's with a man named Floyd, who helped her get her head straight enough to call me. When I talk with him he tells me Floyd is his street name, but his real name is Jeff. He says that he'll get Pam into a methadone program at San Francisco General Hospital later that day and that he believes Pam is serious about wanting to quit. He gives me his address and two cell phone numbers.

After making calls to arrange a place for Pam in a Detox near us in Virginia, I'm on the next flight I can get to San Francisco. With graying hair, and still probably wearing my chronically sad Pietà face, I settle into a crowded coach seat and start fingering my blue rosary beads. I must look the perfect picture of middle-aged Catholic piety. Just then, an older man leans across the aisle to reassure me that the plane is safe.

What can I say? That I'm not worried about the plane, that I'm actually praying for myself to be calm and firm when I meet my heroin-addicted daughter fresh from a month of living under a bridge in San Francisco, a daughter whom I haven't seen in almost a year and a half? I politely say "thank you" and return to my beads. Then I turn my attention to preparing my lesson plans for an upcoming Pathwork training in Brazil which Donovan and I are scheduled to begin in a week.

I'm now extremely focused on the task at hand, as I know I have very little time to complete the planning that would normally have occupied this week. I'm excited by the possibility of Pam's getting off the streets, but I'm also cautious. I'm not eager to get my heart burned again on the hot stove of betrayal.

The drive from the airport to the Mission District is short, and my mind is calm. I get off at Cesar Chavez (Army) Street, and soon cross under a bridge. I see the makeshift shelters of maybe twenty people there, and I know this is likely the very bridge that has been

Pam's most recent home. Picturing my daughter among these residents brings the fuzzy impression of her homelessness into sharp Technicolor reality. I continue down Army and turn onto Mission, pausing near the address I've been given.

About ten Mexican men swarm my rental car, for an unknown purpose. At first I think they're offering to show me where to park my car, but then I wonder if their purpose is not so benign. I call Jeff on his cell phone and then I spot him: a tall, thin, somewhat beat-up and sad-faced middle-aged white man with stringy beard and hair. He comes to my car and confirms that the men are all drug dealers and that it was good I didn't let any of them into the car. Jeff directs me to a parking spot.

He and I walk toward a red-brick apartment building, typical public housing. My heart leaps as my eyes lock on a large bleached-blond tattooed girl with a lip ring walking toward us. I'm sure it's Pam and that now the moment is here—we're actually going to make contact. I feel excited, but cautious, shy even. She reaches out her arms in welcome and we hug. She cries, my eyes mist and I choke up.

෨

I have the sensation that I'm meeting my daughter for the first time. I realize I'm more detached now, better able to see who she is instead of seeing her through the rosy filter of who I want her to be.

But she's also different. Her shoulders are heavy, rounded, tough, as though they've been carrying a lot of weight. She looks older and there are a few more tattoos on her body. But the real difference is something in how she's carrying herself; she seems much more solid, more present than I remember.

After talking with Pam for a few hours in Jeff and Karen's apartment I see it: there's somebody home. My words used to go right through Pam. She always seemed distracted, elsewhere, unable to pay attention. Now she's right here with me.

She tells me stories of her life on the streets. I learn that her street name is Zoë. Everyone on the street makes up elaborate false stories about their identities, giving themselves imaginary biographies and constantly revising their stories so as to hide anything real about themselves.

She tells me that she has no shoes and in fact has been barefoot most of the time she's been on the streets in California. She recalls that Donovan was going to buy her shoes when he'd taken her to San Diego on the way to treatment. "But I was so hung up on Adam and so fucked-up on crystal that I just ran away from Dad. Boy, was I dumb." And then with a sweeping hand gesture and a shoulder shrug, she dismisses the entire last year of her life: "Well, I guess it all led to here." She pauses, and then laughs, "Still shoeless."

She lifts up her shirt to show me her biggest new tattoo. Her entire abdomen is covered with letters that were designed by a graffiti artist, and at first I can't discern what the word is. She tells me: TRUTH. This is what she has emblazoned on her belly. She remembers being with this tattoo artist who offered to do his work for free, an offer she wouldn't imagine turning down. She was very high at the time, using her false street name and telling lies as easily as she opened her mouth. But when the tattoo guy asked Pam what word she would like, she thought about the one word Donovan consistently told her was the most important thing in life: TRUTH. Into her world of stealing, lying, cheating, and using drugs, this word was branded forever onto her body.

As she's telling these stories, Pam is articulate, relaxed, funny, and confident. Pam's multiple psychological diagnoses of dissociation, borderline, and bi-polar personality disorders don't seem to fit who she is at this moment. I'm quietly wondering, *How could her dreadful experiences of addiction and street life have produced this transformation?*

And then it hits me: she's survived. Some fundamental strength has been born in her that wasn't there before. She survived on the tough streets of D.C., in the backwoods of Mississippi, in the parks for the homeless in San Diego, on the mean streets of L.A., and most recently under a bridge in San Francisco. She's made it through her own personal drug war alive. I suspect there are very few of us who could do what she has done. I can't help feeling a secret admiration for her strength and survival skills.

Nothing I'd ever read about addiction or about the horrors of life on the streets prepared me for the reality I'm seeing now. Pam seems saner than she was before she started her downward spiral with drugs. In fact, she may be saner than I've ever seen her. She's here; she's landed on the planet at last.

I'm thrilled to be with her.

❧

After a few hours spent talking with Pam and Jeff and Karen in their apartment, Pam and I go out to a nearby Mexican restaurant, where she eats like she's hasn't eaten in weeks (which is largely true). Back in the apartment, I notice that Pam disappears into the hallway with Jeff a few times, and I finally figure out that they're smoking pot.

Jeff and Karen use methadone and marijuana daily. Given the level of their previous addictive behavior, they consider themselves clean. When I ask Pam and Jeff directly if they're smoking weed, Jeff answers by inviting me to smoke with them.

I consider his invitation. I have smoked marijuana occasionally, but have never been drawn to it. I hate smoking anything (my father had lung cancer). Nonetheless, I say yes to having a puff with them. In the end it seems right to join these new friends, and not be Miss Goody Two-shoes. Probably because I use marijuana so rarely and also because of my many experiences with *Daime,* I find that smoking their weed immediately expands my consciousness. I feel my heart very open to these two lost and struggling life-long addicts. I'm sitting in a wide open space of loving presence.

I invite and hear more of Jeff's life story, including his growing up very poor in the backwoods of Arkansas and his terrible family troubles. He wants to find a spiritual path, but says he can't do Narcotics Anonymous because they're too strict for him. (NA's definition of "clean" would certainly not be the same as Jeff's!) I feel sad as I notice that Jeff always talks about himself as a loser and an addict; he does not seem to have access to a larger, more compassionate view of himself. But all I say is that I respect him very much for all he has been through and for his longing to find God.

Pam and I get the munchies and I suggest going out for ice cream, but Jeff laughs at me, "You wouldn't survive two blocks around here at night. It's way too dangerous a place for a nice middle-class middle-aged lady like yourself." I chuckle and accept his superior wisdom about the streets.

Then Pam and I settle down for bed in Jeff and Karen's small living room—me on the couch, Pam on the floor. We talk and hold hands until we fall asleep, both so relieved to be together again.

✣

The next morning it's time to get serious.

"Pam, if you really want to stay clean, you're going to have to go into treatment."

"Mom, I don't need that shit. I already know what they're going to say. I've been to a bunch of rehabs."

"Not long enough for it to work."

"But it's just the same old stuff. I'm really through using now. I never want to go back to the streets. I'm done. But I sure as hell don't want to be lectured at by anyone."

I take a deep breath and say what needs to be said, "You can't fight this disease alone, Pam. It's too powerful. I have already reserved a place for you at a detox in Virginia. If you aren't willing to go into treatment, then I will not take you back to the East Coast."

Pam pleads, "I just want to drink *Daime*, Mom, that's the only thing that has ever really helped me."

"Pam, if there were a treatment center that encouraged you to drink *Daime*, I'd take you there in a minute. But so far as I know there isn't one. So you'll have to do conventional treatment first to get clean, and then we'll see about drinking *Daime*. The church isn't equipped to deal with addicts, Pam. It's a church, not a treatment center. Anyway I think drinking *Daime* is a privilege, one you'll have to earn by staying clean for a while."

Pam looks sullen, says nothing.

Making an inner prayer to the gods of Al-Anon, I summon the courage to say, "This is my bottom line, Pam. If you aren't willing to go into treatment, I will go back without you. I mean it. You can stay here and get clean on your own."

Jeff comes to my rescue. "Pam, don't be an idiot. You've got a great mom who's tryin' to help you. That's a lot more than I had. C'mon, girl, do what you need to do. She's givin' you a chance here, a chance I never had. Believe me, you're not goin' to be able to stay clean livin' in this sorry city."

"Okay," Pam replies, "but I don't want to get sent away someplace again."

"This detox is close to us. We'll visit you as often as we can."

She shrugs. "I'll give it a try."

"That'll do."

We walk to PayLess to buy shoes and then to a cheap clothing outlet to buy an outfit suitable for the trip. On our walk through the Mission District we retrace Pam's personal trail of tears: She points out the best places for panhandling, where she bought drugs, and where she solicited tricks. It's a neighborhood of sad stories.

Then I drive Jeff and Karen to the local food bank and to the hospital where Karen gets her HIV levels checked. As we pause at a stoplight, Jeff points out a pathetic-looking middle-aged skinny white lady meeting a black man on the corner. We watch as they head into a cheap hotel. Jeff says pointedly to Pam: "She'll probably get ten bucks for that—just enough for her next fix. That'll be you, sister, if you don't get out now."

The next day Pam and I are at the San Francisco airport, which is still in the throes of post-9/11 panic. I've had the presence of mind to bring her passport for ID, as of course she's lost any she had in San Diego. Even in her new traveling outfit, there's still no way Pam can look normal in an airport during this paranoid time. So she's frisked and searched and made to stand in lines… but we eventually get through and onto our plane.

ᔌ

Pam writes:

Jeff and Karen were the angels in my life just when I needed them. I know in my heart that there is a reason I was protected as much as I was. So many people I knew have died, have never gotten out. Jeff and Karen happened to be clean and ready to help someone that day when I was sitting outside Walgreens. Two years later they would both relapse and lose their apartment and their phones, so I lost contact with them. I expect by now they are dead. But that day they helped me, a fellow addict, begin my journey to sobriety. Imagine that.

CHAPTER 23

What Will Work?

Virginia, December 2001 – November 2002

PAM'S off the streets, saying she wants to get clean. But even if she detoxes and gets the drugs out of her system, it's not going to be easy for her to *stay* clean. Even though she is saner than she was, she's still going to have to address all those psychological issues that landed her in the streets in the first place. And to do that, she's probably going to have to submit to a structured treatment program, which she hasn't been able to do up until now. Her two years of surviving on the streets, with no rules or structure whatsoever, haven't necessarily made her any more ready for treatment. Getting Pam out of the streets is going to be easier than getting the streets out of Pam. What will it take?

🦋

Pam enjoys Detox this time. There she meets a recovering addict whose path for staying clean is his daily devotion to the fellowship of Narcotics Anonymous (NA). Kyle goes to or leads an NA meeting every day, sometimes twice a day. He becomes both an inspiration and a friend to Pam.

After Detox, Pam enters New Horizons, a conventional three-month treatment program in Northern Virginia, but only lasts there a little over three weeks. She gives it her best—filling notebooks with her answers to all the traditional questions about her drug history, relapse triggers, anger management issues, and so on. It's a typical regimented program, with immediate consequences for any infraction of the rules, including a rigorous code of cleanliness.

Eventually Pam's refusal to accept rules she doesn't understand or agree with causes clashes with the authorities. She smokes in a no-smoking area one too many times and she's kicked out. They recommend she apply for long-term treatment, which she's unwilling to do.

She ends up on Kyle's couch where she lives for several months staying clean through sheer force of will, going to lots of NA meetings with him, hoping to follow his model of staying clean on his own. She works at a Blockbuster movie store, struggles alone with the inner split between her "bad girl" and "good girl," and has to navigate her intense emotional ups and downs.

At the treatment center the counselors told her she probably has bi-polar disorder, but she was not given medication because the prevailing wisdom is that you can't get an accurate psychiatric diagnosis until the patient is clean and sober for six months. But of course it's very hard to stay clean and sober if you are dealing with constantly fluctuating moods without medication. The temptation to self-medicate with street drugs is strong. Pam's internal chemistry is seriously out of whack, but no one is willing to give her the immediate medication she needs to help her maintain a balanced emotional state.

Pam asks frequently about returning to the *Daime*. But the nearby *Daime* church group leaders are reluctant, agreeing with me that she needs to get more stable in her sobriety first.

❧

By June Pam's been holding on to her sobriety for about five months, and with some trepidation Donovan and I set off for two weeks of teaching in Brazil. I call Pam daily; sometimes we connect and sometimes there's only static on the line. Thousands of miles and a universe away, I feel the fraying rope holding Pam to sanity slowly slipping out of reach. My powerlessness over her disease could not be more graphic; I am talking to my daughter in suburban Virginia from the middle of Brazil. Daily I can feel her sliding back into her street-addict mentality. During my next call Pam tells me she is furious at Kyle, who's accusing her of using drugs.

As soon as I get off the phone I know she's relapsed. And Kyle won't let her stay if she's using. So it's only a matter of time before she'll be back on the streets.

ॐ

Shortly after we return from Brazil Pam calls: "I'm sorry Mom. I just couldn't do it. I'm broke and homeless and back at Dupont Circle. I spent last night with Billy Bob."

"He's clean now. He told me to call."

"I'm glad you're alive."

"Mom, I really missed you so much."

"Pam, I'm sorry. I didn't realize your recovery was so fragile. I'm so sorry."

I hear her crying softly at the other end.

"I want to come home. I can do it. I want to get clean, but I need to be near you, I need to be in a safe place. Will you let me come home now?"

I feel a stab in my heart, but my head clearly recalls the failure of my effort, a few years earlier, to live with her in an apartment so she could get clean, and the intense defeat I felt when she ran away. I know I can't try that again, so I say what I need to say.

"Pam, we can't run a treatment center in our house. It's too hard. I just can't do it. But it does seem like you can't stay clean on your own. Maybe you really do need long-term treatment. I'll be around to support you as much as I can. Do you want the number for Detox so you can start the admission process?"

"No." Long pause. "I love you."

"I love you too Pam."

❧

Two months later Pam shows up at Kyle's and tells him she wants to go back to New Horizons; she really wants to stay clean and doesn't know any other place to go.

At her request I go with her and we talk together with George, the head of the program. She speaks honestly about her life now: living with a violent drug dealer who pushed her against the wall with a knife at her throat, doing lots of crack cocaine, also crystal and sometimes heroin, and turning tricks for drug money.

George goads her a little by suggesting she still has a few months on the street left in her. She agrees with his assessment that she gets bored with being "good." She tells us how she had started stealing movies before she got fired at Blockbuster.

George gets serious. "I just hope you come in before you get killed, Pam. I'm scared for you now that you're involved with the big guys."

"Pam's always pushed the edge of danger," I intervene.

"And you're always there for her," he chides. "You're always the good guy." Then with a slight sneer, he adds, "Always Mommy. But you've got your head in the sand, Mommy. This girl's flirting with real danger this time. No more poor misguided teenager; this is serious stuff."

Pam finally asks, "Can I start again in the New Horizons program?"

"No," he answers authoritatively. "I think you really need something more long-term, and probably the best bet would be our dual-diagnosis long-term treatment program. I'll put you on the waiting list when you are serious. Call me in a week if you still want to come in."

By the time I leave her at Kyle's later that day, Pam's already arranged a ride back to her drug scene at Dupont Circle.

As we part, she tells me, "I'm sorry I got your hopes up."

🐾

My godson Christopher has just been released from prison. He's been in a North Carolina jail for four years this time, for theft and crack cocaine distribution. Now, at age forty-five, he's got his first real shot at making a life for himself. He's earned a GED and been given job training in prison, and he knows he faces another mandatory nine years if he doesn't stay clean and find employment.

I meet him at the Richmond, Virginia bus station to drive him back to his brother's house in Washington D.C. When I tell Chris about Pam's relapse back to the streets of D.C., he gets very agitated and immediately vows to talk to every dealer he knows to track her down. I try to dissuade him from this reckless plan, as I know his own sobriety is fragile and he'll be no use to anyone if he relapses. But he's determined to help me locate Pam and convince her to get back into treatment. They've met more than a dozen times over the years, during some of his rare periods of being free and sober. Pam respects Chris. He's street-smart and open-hearted. He thinks she'll let him help her. We'll see.

After our unsuccessful visit to New Horizons treatment center, Pam calls only occasionally, just to tell me she's alive and to hear my voice. We always exchange "I love you," but we have nothing more to say to each other.

Then one day Chris calls me saying urgently, "Hang on and don't say anything." He gets Pam on the other line and they talk; she doesn't know I'm listening. Pam tells Chris how much she misses me and how upset she feels that I won't have anything to do with her until she's ready for treatment.

Afterwards, Chris urges me to call her, asking me to trust him, saying that every addict needs more than anything to have someone who believes in him/her, someone who is willing to stay connected and keep loving, no matter what. He's been there. He knows.

So I break my own rule of not initiating contact and call Pam. She really wants to talk and is very relieved at my calling. We talk about her options. She says she wants to get clean, but adds, "I can't do another 'behavior modification' thing. I can't stand those rules."

"I'm sorry, Pam. But any place you go there's going to be rules. I hate to say this, but maybe you'll have to suffer even more on the streets until you're humble enough to live by somebody else's rules."

"Maybe. But it makes me crazy."

"Pam, you're living a pretty crazy life now. Do you really think treatment would make you crazier?"

"I can't explain it Mom, but I just can't do it. I'm sorry. I love you."

"I love you too, Pam."

🦚

I'm stumped. She can't do conventional treatment, because she's so resistant to institutional rules. She can't stay clean on her own like Kyle, even with his support and help. The *Daime* community here is not strong enough to take on someone with her level of psychological and addiction issues. And I can't have her using our house as her treatment center. What's left?

Then it hits me. In traditional treatment programs addicts are defined by their personal defects and pathology: their personality disorders, traumas, and addictions. Even though there is constant lip service to a "higher power," conventional treatment is not based on a deep spiritual or holistic understanding. It is based instead on equating the person with their personal psychology.

At the Chapel School and at every treatment center since then Pam has been defined by what's wrong with her and not seen as who she essentially is. When she's herded into a confining corral and branded by the authorities as sick and wrong, she shrinks back into that limited identity. She becomes in her own mind "just another crazy addict," losing touch with her essential humanity and her soul. And this, understandably, makes her feel even more insane.

Her experiences in the *Daime* showed Pam that she is not defined or limited by her craziness; it is simply a sickness her soul is carrying.

A true spiritual perspective views the sick person through the eyes of love. It's the way Jesus saw the sinners as children of God. It's how Mother Theresa saw the lepers in India, as Christ in another guise. It's how Gandhi, Nelson Mandela and the Dalai Lama saw their oppressors—not as "others," but as brothers.

I'm not saying that treatment centers should be staffed only by the likes of Mother Theresa or Nelson Mandela, but that it is possible to embrace this larger, more compassionate picture of human beings when viewing the sick addict, rather than define them by their sickness alone.

Behavior modification—the attempt to change people from the outside with rewards and punishments, which seems to be standard practice in all treatment protocols—has never worked for Pam. It didn't work to change her regressive behavior after the abuse incident when she was four years old, and it failed miserably when she was a rebellious adolescent. I've come to believe that Pam's behavior will only change from the inside—when she is ready, when she can live from her own authentic center—and not from the expectations or punishments other people impose on her.

So many authorities, including me, have tried to break Pam's strong will—from her third grade teacher who relentlessly drilled her on multiplication tables, to the Chapel School staff who punished her by wrapping her in blankets sealed with duct tape. Each time her rebellion and defiance only deepened. This pattern earned her yet another negative psychological label: an "oppositional-defiant personality."

As I ponder Pam's negative response to treatment, I remember that I felt the same way toward the addiction expert Steve who defined me as a "turbo-codependent." It was a constrictive, punitive definition of who I was, and it made me feel crazy and confined. Feeling terribly wrong and bad about myself, I spent most of my time either succumbing to or fighting against this definition of me. I only got sane when I shook myself free from that shackle and found my own inner truth.

So that's what Pam means. She can't be in a place that sees her only as a crazy addict, or she risks going back into believing that definition of herself. She needs a place where her worth is not defined by what she does but by who she is—where her intrinsic inner worth can be seen and respected—and where she can work on her defects, traumas and addictions without being forced to believe that these define her.

Finding a treatment center with an enlightened spiritual approach like this is going to be a tough job, but at last I feel I know what she needs. She needs something way outside the "box" of conventional treatment.

But does such a place exist?

CHAPTER 24

Waiting in Faith

Washington, D.C., December 2002

I KNOW better than to push any help until Pam is ready, until she wants to stay clean badly enough to do whatever it takes. But I'm also determined to find the right place for Pam when that time comes. In this I am defying both my new, very tough-minded Al-Anon sponsor and my old therapist—both of whom feel I should leave the job of finding the right treatment center to Pam. But I know that finding an alternative treatment program is not something she could do right now. I can and will do this for her... experts be damned.

I start my research. There are hundreds of treatment centers in the U.S. Most of them promise a spiritual approach, but there's no telling what they mean by that promise. The Chapel School—where Pam had been for more than two years and which promised to put spirit first— turned out to be both rigid and ineffective. I talk to a dozen different places but nothing clicks for me.

Then I find out about some places outside the U.S. which use *ayahuasca* in the treatment of addiction. Near Mapiá in the Brazilian Amazon a Spanish doctor is combining psychological treatment with the *Santo Daime*. I also read about Takiwasi, a center for treating drug and alcohol addiction, located in the upper Peruvian Amazon, which has a much better recovery rate than conventional treatment centers. It was founded in 1992 by a French doctor who wanted to offer a treatment protocol that would incorporate the ceremonial use of *ayahuasca* from the Peruvian shamanic tradition. I think these programs have the right mix, but they are out of reach geographically.

Then I learn about *ibogaine*. Extracted from the iboga root which is sacred to the indigenous people of Gabon, Africa, *ibogaine* has many of the properties of other native sacraments including opening a connection to spirit and helping to expose the deep inner roots of outer sickness, including addiction. It also has another unique feature, one that was discovered accidentally by a heroin addict who used the plant in the 1970s. It lifts craving for narcotics for a limited period of time, long enough for the addict to get into whatever treatment they need for their underlying issues. This "side effect" has been crucial for the healing of many addicts who have used *ibogaine* in their recovery.

I find out that there is an underground use of *ibogaine* in this country for addiction treatment--especially in Harlem, where African-American addicts can easily relate to the plant's African origins. There is more extensive and accepted use in Holland, Canada, and Mexico. Then I read about an experimental U.S. government-sponsored research project for giving *ibogaine* to drug addicts, headed by Dr. Deborah Mash of the University of Miami.

I call her immediately. We have a wonderful hour-long talk, and she sends me an article about *ibogaine* and its use in Africa. I'm amazed to read of the parallels between the African Bwiti cult which uses *iboga* as its sacrament and the Amazonian *Santo Daime* church which uses *ayahuasca*—even though each religion grew up in entirely different cultures, and their sacraments come from very different plants. Both religions are admixtures of Christian and native traditions. Both regard their sacrament as similar to the wine that Christ gave his disciples so that they could remember him. Both interpret this to mean that these sacred plants can open us to remember our essential spiritual nature, or the Christ-consciousness within us. Both ceremonies involve singing, dancing, and Christian prayers.

Ibogaine is legal in the U.S. in the context of this program run by

Dr. Mash. I am convinced that this is the next step for Pam. Now at last I have something substantive to offer her… when she is ready.

✎

It's Christmas Eve day—snowy, wet, cold. Chris has learned that Pam's left the apartment of her drug dealer. The dealer is accusing her of stealing drugs and money from him and is threatening to kill her. Chris also talks to Billy Bob, her former meth dealer, who says Pam was last seen on the streets of suburban Virginia.

I drive from the house of my ninety-four year old mother in the Maryland suburbs to a police station in Fairfax, Virginia to file a missing person report for Pam. I feel like a grim, grey grinch at this police station where the Christmas party atmosphere is all gaiety and good cheer. It takes a couple of hours before anyone will talk to me, and when I finally tell my story, the stout policewoman tells me there's nothing she can do.

I'm missing Pam terribly. Christmas was always a time of closeness in our family. No matter what else was going on, Pam would warm to us on this special day.

Tonight I'm determined to have a little Christmas spirit with what's left of my family. Neither my mother nor my husband seems to care about having a Christmas tree, but I'm adamant. I've asked Donovan to bring up from our house some of our Christmas decorations, including the lights which go on the tree first. I go out on this snowy night alone and purchase a tree, which I struggle to get standing upright in its metal holder. When I'm ready to decorate the tree I open the box Donovan has brought and discover that he did not bring the Christmas lights. He brought the wrong box.

I tip over the edge. I yell at Donovan, "Why didn't you bring the lights? I told you to bring the lights!" I'm hysterical, and start sobbing. And then I hear the sounds of a walker methodically bump-bumping toward the living room. My mother's coming out from her back bedroom to see what is the matter. The last thing I want to deal with is my mother's upset on top of my own distress. When I broke down in her house two years ago, her response was to want to call 911. She can't deal with emotions, and, really, I don't want to scare her. So I duck into the kitchen and close the door. Then I hear the thump-thump of her walker coming toward the kitchen. I race out the other kitchen door and go back to the living room. She thump-thumps her way to the living room, and I just stand there, frozen like a deer in headlights.

My old mother trundles her walker over to the couch, lets herself fall to a seat, and with a kind but authoritative gesture, motions me to sit down beside her. I obey. She puts her arms around me and pulls my head onto her bony shoulder. I let go, falling into her frail body, weeping.

She's very rarely spoken to me about Pamela. I've also been reluctant to talk with her because years ago I heard only judgments and criticisms about Pam. But now she says, "I don't know what to do. I wish there was more I could do." Between sobs, I reply, "What you're doing right now is perfect."

My mother adds, "I don't know how you stand the pain. You're so strong. I love you so much." Her words astonish and soothe. I relax further and let myself be held in a way that I may never have been held by her, at least not since I was a small child with a skinned knee. Whatever remnants of bitterness I might have been holding onto for all of my sixty-three years now melt completely.

The crying quiets and we are just there, woman to woman, bearing together what I no longer have to bear alone. She reaches her hand toward the walker and grabs her purse by the straps, pulling it toward her. Out of her purse she pulls her credit card, passes it to me, and says, "Go to the drug store and buy some lights. We're going to have the Christmas tree you want."

🏵

Pam writes:

It's Christmastime, but what do I care? As always when I'm using, I only care about one thing: where to get my next drugs. Tony, the small-time dealer I'm living with, gives me an eight ball[1] to sell, and Homer—our gay dealer—has given me another one. Homer wants to help me out because he knows that Tony makes me sell the meth and then he keeps the money. The last time I tried to hold onto the money, Tony almost strangled me to death. Another time when I lied about the money Tony got out his knife. I learned that you tell the truth when you've got a knife to your throat.

This time I think I have a chance to actually make some money. (Yeah, right.) I take Tony's eight ball and put it in baggies on top of a plate. It's a very delicate task because out of every bag I make I have to take out a little bit—just the right amount, not to be obvious—for my own use. I am already high and end up dropping a bunch of the meth on the bathroom floor. This instantly makes it unsellable, as I sell to uppity gay people in the clubs and they will never buy their beloved drug if it has dirt in it.

Oh well, I'll figure it out after I do more meth. I get higher and higher. I am very high and this guy in the house says he has some meth too and we can put it together to make up for the lost meth.

I say instead, "Let's just go to a hotel and worry about it later." So that's what we do.

Before long I'm under the bed in the hotel room, pulling the bottom of the bed apart looking for something that can never be found because it is all in my head. I go to the bathroom and pull the toilet apart, trying to get a good piece of metal to scrape

---

[1] A quantity of crystal meth.

the caulk off the tiles. I know there has to be something behind
the tiles, in the mattress or under the carpet. It is a crazy, drug-
induced illusion but it is very intense, and I end up destroying that
hotel room.

Sometime later I find myself in a strange house where two
drag queens live with a black lesbian who has a crack addiction
and a scary past. She spends a long time telling me about being
kidnapped at age eleven, and held captive and tortured for eight
years. She spooks me out, but I don't pay too much attention
because I'm busy worrying how I can get high again. She won't
give me any of her crack. Finally one of the queens gives me a
small amount of crystal and I go to the bathroom to inject it.
It isn't nearly enough, but it's something.

I look in the bathroom mirror and watch my head start turning left then right, then left then right, over and over. *No. No.
No.* The word is screaming through my head. I'm close to really
losing it. Then something wakes up: *No! NO!! No more. Enough.*
I've got to stop this insanity. I've got to get out of here. But I can't
go back to Tony—he'll kill me for sure. I can't go back to rehab or
my parents' house because they won't have me. I've got only one
option left. I call Kyle.

ᔕ

The day after Christmas I drive to Dupont Circle to meet Chris at
the 3rd Precinct police station. My mother's mellowness has extended
to Chris. As I'm leaving she asks, "How's my god-grandson?" I feel so
close to her and so grateful for her kindness.

Chris and I are going together to file another missing person
report on Pam. These officers take us seriously and immediately send
a policeman with us to check out the house where Chris says he'd
last seen her. Tony answers and says he knows Pam and that she
owes him money. So, now we know that the story Pam told Chris

is probably true.

On our way back to the 3rd Precinct, Kyle calls me saying that Pam has just called him and wants to come to his house to get clean. So, now we know she's no longer a missing person. While we are waiting for the officer to fill out his papers, Kyle calls again and says Pam has called back and asked him to come get her at 15th and Massachusetts, very near where Chris and I now are. I offer to pick her up if she's willing. In five minutes we are at the address.

Pam is, once again, barefoot. It's late December. Her clothes are disheveled and her face is haggard. On the way to Kyle's she tells us how her dealer tried to kill her, strangling her, and it took five people to get him off. Chris says quietly that if he'd wanted to kill her, he would have.

Back at Kyle's house I tell Pam about the *ibogaine* program. The next day she calls and has an hour-long intake interview with a nurse from Dr. Mash's Healing Visions program. We register her for the next program to be held in St. Kitts—a Caribbean island nation near Florida. It strikes me as typical of our culture's ambivalence about drugs that this is a government-sponsored study, but they won't let the research take place on U.S. soil.

CHAPTER 25

Recovery and Relapse

St. Kitts, Florida, and Virginia, January 2003 – June 2004

I N the Miami airport on her way down to St. Kitts, Pam is joined by two other addicts—well-off trust-fund kids also on their way to the *ibogaine* program—who immediately offer her some heroin. "Last chance," they tempt. Pam rejects the invitation, and only then realizes how strongly she wants, at last, to be free of her addiction.

The St. Kitts program is anyone's idea of heaven on earth—beautiful tropical setting, marvelous food, caring professional staff. Pam can hardly believe her good fortune—in serious danger on the streets of D.C. one day and in paradise the next. And she didn't even have to die to get there.

Most important for Pam is the great respect and true caring she feels from the therapists running the program. They recommend she immediately be put on medication for bi-polar disorder which, over the next weeks, will help stabilize her so she doesn't have to deal with the mood swings which in the past have often precipitated relapse.

Dr. Mash and others are genuinely interested in hearing about Pam's experiences with *ayahuasca*—what she learned and how she grew from her connection to this sacred tea. This is certainly a first for Pam. Every other treatment program either disregarded her past work with *ayahuasca* or worse, considered it part of her drug life. Since Pam knew otherwise, this always created a wall between her and those trying to help her.

The *ibogaine* is administered in a medical setting, very different from its original religious use (and different from her use of *Daime*). Nonetheless, she finds it brings her back to the essential learning she did within the *Daime* church ceremonies: affirming her inherent worth, underlining the importance of her connection to God for her recovery, encouraging her to let go of her terrible guilt and self-judgment and instead see her sickness with compassion.

Pam opens up fully and honestly in the groups, and makes an especially good connection to one of the therapists. Not only does she feel respected and understood, but she's also seen as knowledgeable about how sacred plants can help an addict. She does more good therapy in two weeks at St. Kitts than in all her previous attempts.

Pam also discovers what others before her have found: *ibogaine* lifts the craving for narcotics—not permanently, but for long enough that she can begin to focus on her recovery. This window of freedom from cravings is an extraordinary side effect of this substance.

Dr. Mash strongly recommends that we follow up with treatment at G&G Holistic Addiction Treatment Center, run by former addict John Giordano in N. Miami Beach, Florida.[1] John is one of the few addiction professionals who completely supports Dr. Mash's research work with addicts and *ibogaine*. He also is respectful of Pam's experience with *ayahuasca*.

❧

Holistic turns out to be a godsend. Pam stays there for a full year of treatment.

---

[1] G&G Holistic Addiction Treatment Center in N. Miami Beach, Florida, is the only facility Pam attended which is identified by its actual name.

In Pam's words:

Holistic changed my life. I had been to treatment centers all over the country, and I never really got a lot from the programs because all they focused on was rules. I never understood why it was such a big deal if the mirror had a little streak on it, or there was dust on one of the cabinets. At most treatment centers these minor things were made into huge deals, making it difficult to work on the real issues at hand.

It is such a nice atmosphere at Holistic. We wake up every morning with a check- in group instead of a clean-up drill. What a relief! John Giordano spends time with us and laughs with us. I feel like he is someone who looks at me, not down at me.

The whole idea of holistic treatment is to work on body, mind, and spirit, and that is what they do. We have acupuncture and do karate. We are given meds and vitamins. We have daily group sessions that are never too long. Most treatment centers insist you sit for a lot longer than most addicts can bear; that means we lose focus, then get agitated and shut down. Not at all helpful.

We have weekly trips to the spa where we can exercise, relax and have a good time. This helps us recover from torturing our bodies with drugs. We have picnics at the beach, helping us learn to have fun without drugs. All this helps us to know that someone believes we deserve all this. I sure didn't think I did. Above all, Holistic shows me I am a worthwhile person, even if I'm a drug addict, ADD, bipolar, and crazy. I am still very lovable and who I am is okay.

John G. believes in me and I really work hard at Holistic—regular therapy and groups, many NA meetings. I even take courses and get my GED. For the first time in my life I feel really good about myself.

❧

A year into sobriety, Pam relapses.

After completing the program at Holistic I have lots of freedom, too much freedom. My other addiction kicks in—my addiction to men. Many of the guys at Holistic come from wealthy
families and I now get attention from men who would never have
looked at me when I was on the streets. The attraction to hot,
wealthy men driving in fast, fancy cars is very strong. I have always been very submissive to men in my life and when these guys
say "jump," I reply, "how high." I quickly succumb to trying to fill
the fantasies I have in my head about this kind of lifestyle—top
notch strip clubs, ten-dollar shots of liquor, $300 an hour escorts.

When my friend Cody drinks too much and blacks out driving
his Porsche, we have to stop on the side of the road. A stripper
friend of his calls his phone and since he's passed out, I pick up.
She immediately comes and we throw Cody into her car and she
takes us both to her home. She has crack cocaine there and that
is the beginning of my fall back into drugs.

I really believe the same old illusion that this time—with
these people who always seem to have enough money to support their addictions—it will be different, and I'll be able to manage drug use.

But that is not how it works for me. Ever. Within a very short
amount of time I'm back on heroin, barely supporting my habit,
and homeless again.

After a year of sobriety, Pam's body is free of drugs, but she still
retains some of the thought patterns of an addict. She gets restless
and bored with being good. She attends the funeral of one of the addicts who had offered her heroin in the Miami airport, who died of
an accidental overdose. This triggers her hopelessness that anyone ever gets free of addiction. When she feels restless or hopeless,
she doesn't notice that she is slipping from the mindset of recovery,

and she doesn't ask for help, so she slides further into her negative thinking. Ultimately what leads Pam into relapse is believing again every addict's central illusion—that she can control her use of drugs.

🕊

Pam is back on the streets, in Miami this time, and I'm back in the rooms of Al-Anon and back with my therapist. "Pam's relapsed," I say to explain my re-appearance in his office. With a sigh, I add, "I should've seen it coming. Her attitude lately has really slipped. All year while she was working the program at Holistic she was humble and grateful pretty much every time we talked. But lately she's been sounding emotionally cut-off, arrogant and willful. Even so, I had on my rose-colored glasses again and missed the clues."

Anticipating the inevitable therapeutic intervention, I add, "I feel kicked in the stomach again. The old bitterness, the familiar anxiety. I really hoped we were done with the drama this time, but no such luck."

"Are you interested now in my offer to get you some help with anti-depressants?" he asks. "You've turned me down in the past, but I wonder if now you might benefit from some medication to help you through this rough spot."

"Thanks, but I don't think so. I've made it this far without them, and I don't expect this passage is going to be any rougher than what I've already been through. Maybe easier. I really know this time that I've done all I could do. There's no more guilt. My part is over. It's be-tween her and God now."

After the session I realize that something deep has shifted. The old impulse to fix Pam seems to have been lifted. The illusion that her fate is up to me seems to have been dispelled. I'm tenderly holding this relapse and its inevitable pain without insisting that anything should be different. I accept that I can't know the end of this story we are living; I can only embrace each chapter as it unfolds. Time and again I have walked the plank blindfolded, been pushed over the edge, and nearly drowned in the horrors of addiction. I have been tossed about by waves of terror and despair, felt myself on the brink of death and of insanity, and yet … not only have I survived, both my heart and my faith have become stronger. Into this faith I will, once again, surrender.

℘

After a couple months on the streets Pam comes back to Virginia and lands on Kyle's couch, trying once again on her own to get clean. By herself she detoxes from heroin. A few weeks later Donovan offers to be with Pam on her birthday to talk about options for treatment. She turns him down, saying she knows from now on it's up to her to figure out how to stay clean.

The night of her birthday, Pam relapses again. Her drug use is now alcohol and smoked crack cocaine—no more injected drugs—but of course she can't stay at Kyle's if she's using. He drives her to a nearby town where she can get into a Salvation Army shelter which will allow her to enter a treatment program for free. She leaves the shelter after two days.

A week later Pam shows up at the door to our house. I spot two Latino boys in the car. She tells us she's drunk and "fucked up" on crack, but badly wants to talk to us. Donovan invites her in and we sit at our round oak kitchen table. Her face is ashen, her clothes disheveled, her hair chopped off. (And of course she's barefoot.) She doesn't seem to be manipulating; she's just simply and genuinely a mess. She's weeping and repeating over and over, "I'm sorry, so, so sorry I failed again. I'm just such a loser. I can't ever do anything right. I'll always be a failure."

"Pam, I'm so sorry this happened." I'm teary and yet remarkably calm. "Of course your relapse upsets you. But remember what they say: relapse is part of recovery."

"You must hate me."

"I don't hate you, Pam. I love you and I always will. Nothing you do can ever change that."

"I'm suicidal, Mom. Really. I don't want to live if I'm just going to keep disappointing everybody."

"Do you have specific ideas about suicide?"

"Yes," the words tumble out, "I wanted to OD on heroin but couldn't find any when I wanted it. I thought about throwing myself in front of a train, but the trains go too slowly through town to kill anyone. I also thought of trying to find a gun or a knife, but then I saw some pictures on a website of mutilated bodies after suicides. I didn't want to end up that way."

Donovan adds, "And then your Mom would have to pick up the mutilated body pieces and put them in a coffin."

I'm swallowing hard, holding my stomach and hoping the calmness remains.

"Yeah, I guess you wouldn't like that."

Donovan affirms, "No, Pam, we wouldn't."

I let his words hang in the air for a minute, then add, "We hope you choose to live. Relapses happen, Pam. Don't let it destroy your faith in yourself. You can start over again."

I'm feeling a little urgent now. I've got one hand reaching out to Pam and one over my heart. Then more words come rushing out of my mouth. "Look, I'll take you to an emergency room. I'm sure we can get some medication to stabilize you, or we can find emergency psychiatric treatment."

"No, no, I just can't do it. Thanks, Mom. Thanks for offering, but I really don't know if I can go on." With her head in her hands, she's sobbing again, "I just can't stand to try again and disappoint you again."

"Pam, this is *your* life we're talking about. I'll survive whatever you do. Remember, this is a terrible, powerful disease you've got. It's trying to take you down now. Maybe it will, maybe it won't. But it's not about disappointing me, that's just the disease talking to try to convince you to give up."

She looks up, and in a sad, plaintive voice says, "I don't know if I'm going to make it, Mom."

I'm praying non-stop. Something in me suddenly relaxes and lets go a little deeper. I stop trying to get Pam to listen to me or do anything at all. I just surrender and accept the truth of what she's saying.

"You know, Pam, you're right. I don't know either if you're going to make it. What I *do* know is that I respect the effort you've given to your recovery. I know it was a struggle and you gave it your best. You were clean and sober for a year. You got your GED. You've worked hard on yourself, facing your issues—at St. Kitts, at Holistic and in the *Daime*. Don't forget what you've already done. … I've also given you *my* best. We've both done the best we could. If this disease ends up killing you, so be it. I accept whatever you need to do. I will never stop loving you."

"Thanks, Mom." She gets up from the table and goes to the door where Donovan and I both give her a hug. She drives away with the two unknown Latino men, to an unknown destiny.

Anyone who's been around serious addiction knows that death is always just around the corner. As an addict once shared with me, "When you walk the path of recovery, you have to step over a lot of dead bodies." So I'm well aware that this time it could be Pam.

CHAPTER 26

Death and the Deathless

Maryland and Virginia, June 2004 – December 2005

PAM writes:
I'm closer to suicide then I've ever been. I'm emotionally worn out. My relapse after a year of sobriety at Holistic devastates me. I fall right back into my belief that I'm a failure at life. I feel that I can't take trying to get clean and failing again.

In the town where Kyle dumped me, hoping I'd go back into treatment, I fall into a new street life in the Mexican community, quickly transferring my Portuguese to Spanish and getting around easily. The Mexican people I meet are poor but real—about as opposite as you can get from the rich, glitzy life in Miami. I have quite a lot of guys who regularly help me out—in exchange for sex of course—but I always have a place to stay. These men never turn me out on the streets. I am always welcome somewhere.

I feel at home in the Hispanic community. I don't know why I have such a sense of belonging here, but I believe it is in my blood. I feel more Latina than Gringa.

I meet my future husband Carlos in a public park at a Mexican picnic. He is there playing soccer and I tell him I like his fancy black truck. He asks me to come eat Chinese with him. After that we go our separate ways—he heads back to his nice apartment, I return to my crack smoking. But he comes and visits me the next day and brings me food to eat. He tells me he can pick me up after he gets off work and we can go to his place.

So that's what I do. We are pretty inseparable after that. He offers to let me stay at his place if I agree to stop using. He is kind. He doesn't push me too hard; he is patient with me. The first few days with him at his apartment he feeds me and even buys me some drugs, so I can come down slowly.

Carlos does not drink or use. I respect him. He has an all-night job in a factory. Even when I beg him not to leave me alone, he always goes to work—every night, no matter what. Carlos shows me trust from the beginning. He leaves me with food and the cable TV. The fact that he trusts me to not steal his stuff makes an impact. Again, being treated like a human being, and not just some loser to be taken advantage of, makes a huge difference in my recovery.

Pam calls to tell me she's living with a young Mexican man who's helping her get clean.

"I'm doing it Mom, I haven't used for three weeks now. I guess I just have to do things my own way. I'm so glad for everything I've ever learned, though. It's all helping me a lot now. And I really like Carlos, he's very good to me. I'm happy, Mom."

Maybe I'm just ready. But I think that Carlos sees something in me and I in him, and that we help each other. I don't get better overnight, but it's the beginning of the end. It's also the beginning of a very different life. A life with love—true relationships with a man and with my family—with a job and a paycheck, a driver's license, and even a car.

Little by little, Carlos and I fall in love. He tells me about growing up in rural Mexico in a house with a dirt floor, and about walking across the desert at night with other immigrants seeking a better life. I tell him about living in abandoned houses in the black areas of D.C., about sleeping under bridges in California. We enjoy hearing each other's life stories. We have fun together.

Three months later Pam calls to say she's still living with Carlos and she's still clean. What happened? I'm sure it helps that she is with a man who loves her and accepts her as she is. I'm sure it also helps that she is confident of my unconditional love for her.

But what is the crucial element in her being able to stay clean now? How is she finally finding the strength within her to maintain sobriety? Does it help that she really feels done with seeking help from outside herself, so that she is now finding her own way? Or did all the drug rehab she's received—especially her full year of treatment at Holistic—suddenly click inside her? Are all the teachings she's been given in the *Daime* now available to her? What woke up to help her do what she has never been able to do before?

I ponder these questions daily and keep discovering: I don't know any more about her recovery than I've ever known about her addiction. I guess, as she says, she was simply ready. And when she was ready, another angel came to help. I hold close the joyful mystery of her apparent recovery, knowing also that relapse is always possible.

🔊

Pam calls to say she would like to come to Maryland and bring Carlos to meet me and her grandma. When I tentatively tell my mother Pam's request, she graciously invites us all to lunch at a nearby restaurant. Pam translates for Carlos, who speaks very little English. Hanging out in the Mexican community these last months, Pam's already talking a blue streak in Spanish.

After lunch my mother and I watch out the restaurant window as Pam and Carlos tumble around on the grass outside like little kids—punching each other, laughing, rolling over top of each other, kissing, then giggling.

"Like puppies," I comment.
"Puppy love," adds my mother, with a wry smile on her mouth.

❧

Seven months later my mother is dying. I have the great good fortune to be with her during most of her last two weeks.

My mother's lifelong anxiety about everything—letting her children cross the street alone brought heart palpitations—seems to have lifted now that she's facing the ultimate fear. She's mostly relaxed and even funny. When I share with her that my sister and I—who have not been close—agree on every detail about the burial and home memorial service, she quips, "Well, that's worth dying for!" When she shares that she's had a vision of a man in a black suit coming to get her, she looks at me, winks and adds, "And he looks just like Elvis!" She gets to say goodbye to all the grandchildren and even waits to die until early morning after I've had a good night's sleep.

At the moment of her passing, I am sitting next to her on the bed Hospice has arranged for us to have in her home.

In the moments after Mom's death, I weep, not so much in grief as in gratitude, because she has let me be fully with her in this most profound of all passages. The personal love I feel for my mother carries me into a transpersonal realm where there is only love—the love that transcends death and personalities. I feel the two of us merging into one consciousness, melting into the inner reality of union behind our outer lives of apparent separation. Relaxing even deeper, the ground of all Being becomes apparent—a space of compassionate awareness, of empty fullness, of vibrant nothingness. I am flooded with the deepest peace I have ever known. It is my mother's final and greatest gift to me.

∾

Pam has now been with Carlos for ten months and is still clean and sober—mostly on her own, but occasionally attending NA meetings when she feels the need.

I've been visiting my grandmother regularly in the last weeks of her life and have been amazed at how much I enjoy being with her and how sweet she is with me. If there is anyone I thought would judge me harshly for the life I have led, I thought it would be her. She is such a proper lady—the one who taught me table manners and expected me to make good grades and go to college. But all I get now from Grandma is simple sweet love, and caring and delight that I am with her.

I get the call that she has passed when I am finishing up my 24-hour shift at the home where I take care of mentally ill adults. I drive immediately up to Maryland to be with my mom.

My grandmother's body is laid out in the bedroom where she died. My mom had engaged the services of a lady who helps people take care of the bodies of their loved ones after death.[1]

I sit for a long time in the living room, too scared to go in to see Grandma's body. Up until that point in my life, death had never perplexed me. I always believed that it was such an inevitable thing that I shouldn't bother contemplating it. But for some reason, being so close to this body that just a few days before had been full of life is very disorienting to me.

All of a sudden I don't understand. But when I go into the bedroom, she looks so beautiful, I just feel peace. I still don't understand—where has Grandma gone? But it's okay. Wherever

---

[1] Beth Knox who runs a service called Crossings (*www.crossings.net*).

she is, peace is there too. I feel I have passed through the wall of death and into the mystery that no one understands.

Our now multi-cultural family travels in a limo to the graveyard where my mother's body will be buried. The pallbearers include Carlos, an illegal Mexican alien soon to be my son-in-law, and Chris, my African-American convicted-felon godson. We don't say prayers because my mother wasn't religious, but we all hang around the gravesite for a while together under the burial tent. Pam and Chris hug each other and cry; they're both missing Grandma already. Carlos stares at the ground in self-conscious silence.

The rest of my well-educated all-white family—including my husband Donovan and my super-competent lawyer sister, her husband, and their three high-achieving children—are also here, honoring my mother in their own way. As we all stand around the coffin poised on top of the hole in the ground, they make fond jokes about my mother's love of grammar. (Is her body lying in the ground? Or has it been—as a newly inanimate object—laid in the ground?)

🙪

A week later Pam—who has only one ovary, has been on birth control pills since living with Carlos, and who has never conceived a child during her many years of outrageous and unprotected promiscuity—finds out she is pregnant. Pam is determined to keep their baby.

Here I am—this no-good drug addict who hasn't done much of anything—all of a sudden about to do the most important thing on earth, giving birth to a soul of the universe. I know right away that I need to embrace the true nature of what is happening. I am now going to be the MOST important person to someone, meaning I have to stop being the most important person to myself.

During my pregnancy I am very attentive to advice given to me. I read books and watch TV shows about giving birth. I go to childbirth classes. With my parents' help, I buy everything that people say I'll need. I love picking out clothes and diapers and butt creams. I also adore feeling my baby grow inside me. When I look at my tummy and see the shape of a little foot poking out, it is so amazing. I have everything ready for my child.

Pam wants to prepare herself for impending motherhood by returning to the *Daime* church, which welcomes her back now that she is drug-free. In Amazonian indigenous cultures, where *ayahuasca* is regarded as a sacred medicine, many pregnant women use this tea both to strengthen their bodies and to align their wills with their new life task as mothers.

We support Pam in her choice to drink *Daime*, which is easier to do now that the use of *ayahuasca* as a religious sacrament is being reviewed by the Supreme Court of the United States. (In February 2006 Justice John Roberts would write his first opinion, in which the Court unanimously upholds the right of the Brazilian UDV church to use *ayahuasca* as its sacrament in the United States.)

Pam participates in a *Daime* ceremony every other week for the remaining months of her pregnancy. She declares to me, "I want more than anything in the world to be a good mother to my baby. I so badly want to be able to give her what I was never given by my birth mother. I'm praying all the time now, Mom, I've never wanted anything more than this. Every time I drink *Daime* I get more confident that I can do it. The *Daime* believes in me."

❧

At a *Daime* ceremony about midway in Pam's pregnancy, I look over at Pam and "see" the soul of her daughter—a strong, intelligent, ancient presence—inviting me to remember my deep connection with her. I have the sensation that all the scattered iron filings of my soul are now lining up with their magnetic true north—total unconditional love.

This unconditional love that has always been calling me pulls me deeper into Itself. In a shift simultaneously subtle yet radical, my perspective on life alters. Rather than being a person experiencing human love, or even a person being called by the Divine Mother to express Her love, the person that I was disappears altogether. The love that pulls me now melts away the sense of being a separate self, like ice dissolving in warm water. There is no room in this love for two. No room for lover and beloved. There is only this One Love, this one reality, expressing as Susan, as Pam, as Pam's unborn daughter, and indeed as all creation. This foundational love wakes up within this body to reveal itself as the truth of what I am.

CHAPTER 27

New Life

Virginia, January 2006

C ARLOS is highly ambivalent about becoming a father, but finally assents to marrying Pam—a week before her due date. Carlos feels too squeamish to be present at the birth, so I go with Pam to childbirth classes. We arrange to have a home birth with Donovan and me present. We have a midwife and our friend Mary Janet, who will be the new baby's godmother. We've also made arrangements with the hospital in case Pam needs to give birth there. We rent a birthing tub to ease the painful contractions of labor.

At eight in the morning Pam's contractions begin. They are mild but consistent that whole day and through the following night. Donovan and I sleep a few hours; Pam does not sleep.

By twenty-four hours into labor, the contractions are coming every three minutes, very intense. Pam gets into the birthing tub and breathes a sign of relief; the water relieves some of the intensity.

The hours drag on as Pam's labor pains intensify. When the midwife checks, her cervix has not dilated. More hours, more pain, still no increase in dilation. Now the anxiety is mounting. I find myself fixated on the thought that we need to have a home birth, no matter what. Noticing this forcing current in myself, I'm aware this is probably not at all what Pam needs. So I recede from my usual helping role and wait to see what will happen next.

Donovan steps in.

Donovan writes:

I can feel Pam's pain, and feel that her distress is increasing. It's been twenty-nine hours already since contractions started. She's giving it her best, and still she doesn't dilate.

I begin leaning on the side of the tub, holding Pam in my arms. Sometimes she cries with the pain, and when she does, I cry with her. I feel her bravery, and I admire her. As time goes on, the last padlocks that I had put around my heart break and fall away. I am not defending my heart from her any longer. I feel wide open to her pain, and it shudders through my body as I hold her.

I can feel her mood shifting; she doesn't say anything but I can sense the difference. She has been determined to have a home birth. Now I can feel that resolve weakening; the pain has gone on for so long, with so little result, that she is starting to give up. Her head has been resting on my arms. She looks up into my eyes—with physical agony and with emotional pleading. I know what she wants.

So I say aloud: "I think we need to take her to the hospital and get her some help for the pain." Pam's eyes, looking into mine, fill with tears, relief and gratitude. I can hear Susan, a few feet away, saying she thinks we could give it a little more time to see if the dilation will come. I immediately say, "No. Pam is already too exhausted."

The professional midwife begins packing up her things and preparing to leave. Since we are now deciding to give up on the home birth, she will not accompany us to the hospital. We get a robe around Pam, and Susan and I and our friend walk her down the steps to our car.

My strong emotional connection to Pamela continues. All of my past resentment toward her falls away. All of my judgemental-ness toward her seems to have melted. I am in great admiration of her: she has given this her absolute best, and has suffered great pain for hours and hours without complaining.

We call ahead to the hospital and they receive us well. At first we are all allowed in the room with Pam as they prepare her for the epidural. The pains keep coming stronger and stronger. Finally the chief nurse says that all of us have to leave except one; Pam could choose whomever she wants to stay with her. I am surprised to hear her say, "I want my dad." Susan and our friend quickly exit the room. The M.D. is slow to arrive and Pamela is getting more and more panicky from the pain. The chief nurse keeps asking her questions in an attempt, I suppose, to distract her. I begin to feel angry about how long it is taking for the anesthesiologist to arrive, but fortunately he comes through the door before I do or say something foolish.

The shot he gives Pam takes effect quickly, and Pam breathes sighs of relief. So do I. I feel a physical wreck myself, so I can only imagine what she must feel like. Then comes the doctor, a woman, who will do the actual delivery.

Pamela is able to rest for a while, and regain some strength. I sit by her side and hold her hand, and tell her I love her and that I am so proud of her.

And then it really is time for the birth. The nurses return, and Susan and Mary Janet rejoin us. Pam is well dilated now. The contractions begin more strongly than before, and everyone encourages her to PUSH. She says that she doesn't know how to push, but we can all see that in fact she does push when she is told to. At last I see the crown of a little head, with lots of thick black hair! I'm standing by Pam's left hand, giving her lots of verbal encouragement. The baby's head comes out a bit farther each time, only to slip part of the way back in at the end of each push. There are two or three times I'm sure it's coming all the way, but then it slips back, and I am so affected that my body twists around and stomps the floor. A nurse gives me a glance of alarm.

At last the baby comes all the way, in a rush, with the doctor receiving her. Huge relief, smiles all around, and I exclaim, "Oh, she's perfect!"

Pam is spent, and anxiously awaiting her baby. The child is weighed and wiped and put on her chest. Pam cries, as do I, as does Susan. The words of an old song come into my mind: "Every time I hear a newborn baby cry, I know why I believe."

Pam writes:

Nothing about the birth of my daughter happens the way I expect or plan. I assumed my mom would be my main support, like she's always been. Instead it is my dad who gives me what I need. I feel more love from him than I have ever felt my whole life.

I arranged to have a home birth. Instead I go to the hospital. Not in the plan. And have an epidural. Also not in the plan.

A lot of the process of growth for me is seeing very clearly: God is in charge here. And that's as it should be. I'm not in charge of life—not my addiction and not the birth of my daughter either. It is all in the hands of a great mystery called God. And that I can trust.

🦢

The love in the birthing room is as palpable as a tropical breeze, as fragrant as lilacs in bloom. Having passed through the long hard winter of dealing with active addiction—years when we were preoccupied with plowing our uncertain paths through blinding storms and chest-deep snows—we are now entering the springtime of our family.

Yet… this love that is so palpable among us now is deeper than a passing season, deeper even than the best human love story. It goes to the foundation of what we are. It is the eternal springtime of spirit beneath the changing seasons of outer appearances; it is the ever-new life force giving birth to all our human stories. It is this essential love which guided me on my rescue mission to Omaha, and which later allowed me to let go of my daughter when she showed up drunk and suicidal at my kitchen table.

This deeper love has revealed itself as my true nature. It is, equally, Pamela's true nature. We are all essentially love incarnate—spirit in human form—with the great privilege of recognizing our oneness.

Pam and I started out on opposite ends of the football field—I was wearing the anxious, controlling good mother mask, she the screwed-up bad kid mask. We kept running at each other's masks and defenses until we both were bloody and beaten. Only then could we meet in the middle of the field—beyond ideas of right and wrong, beyond all our ideas of who we thought we were. Only then could we surrender to the power living within these bodies, a power greater than our limited ideas about ourselves. We began to recognize that our whole drama was orchestrated by love. Love created us, love directed us, and ultimately love triumphed in the recognition of each other as equal expressions of the one enduring life force.

❧

Pam calls Carlos, who shows up in the room minutes later. As she hands their baby to him, her face is glowing. Extending the tips of his fingers, Carlos gingerly accepts this precious package. He's tentative, as though he's just been handed a fragile white porcelain doll belonging to somebody else. Slowly the muscles of his smooth brown arms relax as he receives the warmth of this squirming, pulsing baby girl whose dark hair, brown eyes, and light tan face mirror a paler version of himself. He glances shyly at Pam, "*Ella es bonita.*" (She is beautiful.)

EPILOGUE

Love Unbroken

Virginia, October 2011

PAM now has two children. She lives in a modest two-bedroom apartment close to us. Her five-and-a-half year old Isabela has just started kindergarten; her three year old son Sebastian goes to day care three mornings a week. Pam's husband Carlos is in jail and, when he gets out, he will be deported to Mexico. We visit Carlos when we can, and he calls Pam on the phone frequently.

Pam is now a full-time, single mom to both kids. She takes her parenting job very seriously. At age thirty, Pam is glad to be a grown-up at last.

I'm a fully engaged seventy-two year old grandmother: racing to the emergency room to meet Pam after her son has had a concussion... skipping through the woods with Isabela in search of toads to catch... getting Sebastian dressed in his rubber boots and fireman hat to go visit the fire engines a block away from their house... enduring Isabela's screams as she resists our requirement that she clean up after an art project... collecting acorns from our lawn with Isabela dressed in her full-length black lace dress-up clothes... getting down on the floor with both kids to arbitrate a sibling dispute over Sebastian's new plastic fire truck.

Every weekend Isabela spends a night or more at Donovan's and my house. At night I sing my standard repertoire of bedtime songs, which has remained the same since Bela was born. We always start with our favorite:

I see the moon, the moon sees me. The moon sees the one that
I want to see. So God bless the moon, and God bless me, and God
bless the one that I want to see.
It seems to me that God above created you for me to love. He
picked you out from all the rest because He knew I'd love you best.

And then we pray for every member of our family, and give thanks
for our blessings.

As always, Donovan is the glue that holds the scattered and sometimes ragged pieces of our family together. On the spiritual level, he
quietly radiates to all of us a deep calmness and reassurance. On the
practical level, he earns most of our money and makes sure our bills
get paid. He's the father figure for both grandchildren. Bela comments
on how strong he is, and asks him to be her protector from the mon-
sters she fears lurk in the dark. Donovan assures her that if any monster gets even close to our house, he will punch that monster right in
the nose. Bela seems satisfied.

❦

Pam's a good mom: She exudes an innate lovingness, a comforting warmth, which communicates to her children her unconditional
acceptance. And she's handling her responsibilities well: She gets her
kids to school and doctor's appointments on time, plays imaginative
games with them, walks with them around the neighborhood and to
a nearby park, fixes all their meals, and gets them both to bed early.
She consciously works on improving herself—her bulletin board has
reminders of the mothering skills she's working on, next to inspiring
words of *Daime* hymns. She's a full-time mom now, but aspires to write
more and to get certified to work as an English-Spanish translator.

She longs to visit Brazil again.

Pam's been clean for more than five years of regular drug testing. She's had a couple of slips—one weekend drinking beer, and once smoking pot, but she bounced back from these mini-relapses with renewed determination. She's happily learning, as they say in NA, to "live life on life's terms." Every day her thinking becomes more reliable and her actions more loving.

But of course there's also the inevitable downside: Pamela continues to struggle with serious psychological and medical issues, some of which are the result of her years of physical self-abuse. She's on medication for bi-polar disorder. She struggles with fatigue and joint pain from Hepatitis C. She has frequent headaches and an ulcer. Her son was born with a misaligned foot. Both kids have needed dental surgery. The list goes on.

ॐ

Life keeps giving me opportunities to remember what I've been shown—that outer challenges do not have to be viewed as proof that something is wrong. It is only my thoughts—believing "this shouldn't have happened" or "something is wrong and it's up to me to fix it"— which create frustration and suffering out of life experience. The inevitable difficulties can, instead, be viewed as love's invitation to drop all judgments and defenses, and simply open to whatever is present. When pain is present, I can allow it and let it soften me. This makes space for awareness of the deeper presence holding the pain. I always find that when I am not separating from *what is*, love naturally arises.

This deeper love came to me only when I stopped trying to solve the problem of my daughter, and stopped trying to fix the problem of my pain. As I began to heal from the underlying belief that something was wrong with us, I started trusting the love that was guiding us. I relaxed into accepting the unfolding of Pamela's and my intertwined lives as something inevitable and mysterious, a spiritual journey into the unknown.

By traveling through the horror of my daughter's drug addiction, and meeting it as fully as I was able, a new safety net has been woven. Life is revealing itself as immensely trustworthy, woven of a single, interconnected fabric. Each apparent rending of the fabric—each runaway, each relapse, each failed rescue—which temporarily felt so painful and so wrong, kept driving both Pam and me deeper toward the healing crises that were necessary for total surrender.

Each crisis deepened my faith in that mysterious presence that repairs each apparent tear in the fabric of life, not by eliminating it, but by revealing it as a necessary part of the tapestry's deeper design.

Each crisis stripped away more of my conventional ideas—about addiction and treatment, about motherhood and love, about right and wrong, about life and death, and, most centrally, about who I thought I was. Finally all that remained was the foundational presence of love unbroken. ❧

For More Information, Visit:

www.loveunbroken.org

offering:

A Study Guide
with questions for each chapter. Beyond enriching your reading of *Love Unbroken*, these questions will support you in coming to terms with the disappointments and traumas in your own life.

Advice to Parents
who suspect their child may be abusing drugs. A summary of the steps I went through in my recovery from the family disease of addiction, which then allowed me to be a positive force in my addicted daughter's life.

Background / Resources / Links
Summaries of all the spiritual paths that contributed to my spiritual growth and which are mentioned in *Love Unbroken*, with links to relevant websites.

Photo Galleries

Susan's Bio

A Disclaimer

Love Unbroken speaks favorably about the *Santo Daime* church, the G and G Holistic Addiction Treatment Program, and Dr. Mash's Healing Visions program. I want to make clear that I receive no monetary benefit or any other form of remuneration from any of these organizations.

I am not advocating for the *Santo Daime* and do not consider it a solution for the disease of drug addiction. The *Santo Daime* is a church, not a treatment modality. Most addicts need treatment, and many people find that conventional treatment alone works well for them. Others find that they need an additional spiritual practice or a connection to a church in order to open up or sustain a connection to a Higher Power. Our participation in the ceremonies of the *Santo Daime* church opened up such a connection for us, but our recovery depended also on our participation in various twelve-step programs, on different forms of therapy and on other routes for our healing. The *Santo Daime* church cannot be expected to provide a cure for addiction or any other disease.

Further, the *ayahuasca* experience is not for everyone. Drinking this tea is a serious, non-recreational, undertaking. The physical side-effects can be extremely unpleasant; many people who try *ayahuasca* once never attempt it again. Nothing I say in this book should be construed as recommending *ayahuasca* or the *Santo Daime* path for anyone.

Susan's Acknowledgments

Deepest thanks for the creation of this book go to D. Patrick Miller of Fearless Books who has guided us every step of the way from editing the manuscript through producing the book.

The support of many friends, too numerous to name, was crucial in helping me carry on with this project when I was discouraged, or fearful of the consequences of publication. I received many reassurances about the value of the book and its potential for helping other addicts and other parents of addicts, and for expanding the worldview of those involved in the field of addiction.

I was especially encouraged by many well-respected spiritual teachers who saw in this tale the universal journey from fear to love, from worry to faith, from concern for the particulars of our own stories to awakening to the universal love that lives behind and within all stories.

Nothing about this book, or my life, would be as it is without the undying support of my beloved, my life partner, my spiritual mate, my husband Donovan.

Pam's Acknowledgments

I want to acknowledge everybody who was part of my journey—all the addicts, all the homeless people, even all the dealers. All the drug counselors, rehab centers, and friends in recovery. Everyone played their part; I remember all of you. Even though there may be some people or incidents that might be judged as "bad," I truly understand now that that was not the case. Everything happened for a reason. I now see my addiction as simply the story I had to live until it was done so I could learn what I needed to learn and become who I am today. Today my eyes and my heart are open. I see the incredible beauty and love that are always here, even in moments of darkness, pain, and loss.

I have enthusiastically joined my mother in telling our story because I truly believe it will help many addicts and their families who are still suffering from this disease.

I am grateful to the *Daime* which was the way God came to me to show me that I was worthwhile and lovable, even when I didn't believe in myself. I give thanks to my husband Carlos and to my children, whose love helped me to get and stay sober. I am grateful for my adoptive parents, my real parents, without whom nothing about my life would be as it is—then or now.

Made in the USA
Charleston, SC
23 April 2012